The world is in peril.

A long-forgotten evil has risen from the far corners of Erdas, and we need YOU to help stop it.

Claim your spirit animal and join the adventure now:

1. Go to scholastic.com/spiritanimals.
2. Log in to create your character and choose your own spirit animal.
3. Have your book ready and enter the code below to unlock the adventure.

Your code:

N2HNPHXWX9

By the Four Fallen,
The Greencloaks

scholastic.com/spiritanimals

The surface of the lagoon
began to tremble and shake.

Moving sinuously, the Great
Lion emerged at the far side.

SPIRIT ANIMALS™

RISE AND FALL

Eliot Schrefer

SCHOLASTIC INC.

Arctica
EUR
Trunswick
Greenhaven Castle
Concorba
Okaihee
AMAYA
N

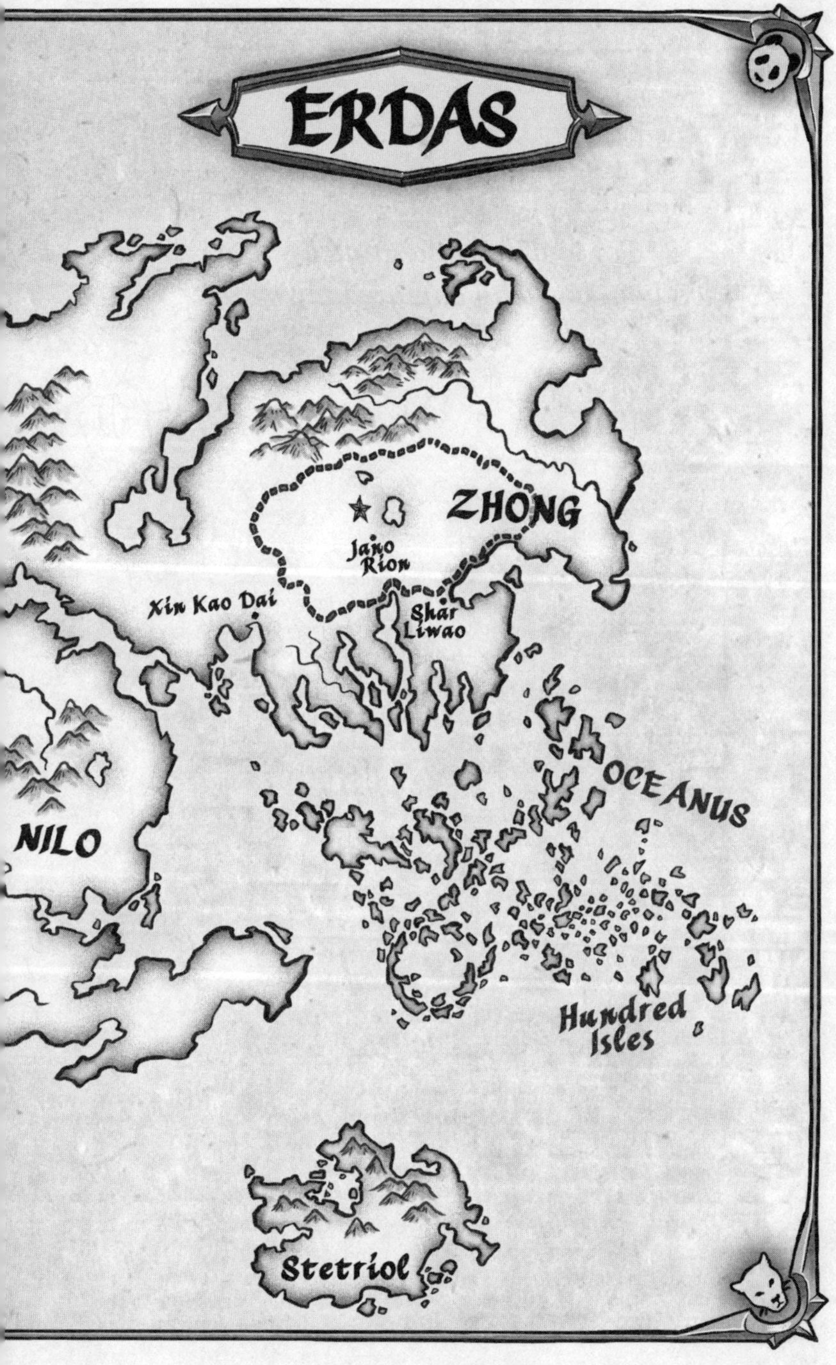
ERDAS
ZHONG
Jano Rion
Xin Kao Dai
Shar Liwao
OCEANUS
NILO
Hundred Isles
Stetriol

For Ombwe and Oshwe,
two bonobos who captured my spirit
–E.S.

Library of Congress Control Number: 2013953382

ISBN 978-93-5103-697-5

12 11 10 9 8 7 6 5 4 3 2 1 15 16 17 18 19

Map illustration by Michael Walton
Book design by Charice Silverman

First edition, January 2015
Reprinted by Scholastic India Pvt. Ltd. : January 2015, Sept. 2015
Printed at Batra Art Press, New Delhi

Scholastic US: 557 Broadway • New York, NY 10012
Scholastic Canada: 604 King Street West • Toronto, ON • M5V 1E1
Scholastic New Zealand Limited: Private Bag 94407 • Greenmount, Manukau 2141
Scholastic UK Ltd.: Euston House • 24 Eversholt Street • London NW1 1DB

1

PRISONERS

THUD!

Abeke startled awake, shivering. At first she thought she'd dreamed the noise. Then she heard it again.

THUD!

Abeke leaped, nearly knocking her skull against the ceiling. The chain fastened to her ankle slammed against Meilin, waking her.

"What is it?" Meilin asked, groping in the dark.

Abeke groggily remembered where they were: still imprisoned in the brig of a ship, on their way to the Conqueror camp in southern Nilo. Abeke had once before found herself on a Conqueror ship just like this one – only on that journey she'd been a guest of honor. She'd had a feather bed, a mirror framed in gold, and had been allowed to roam wherever she liked. She hadn't been locked in the brig, a tiny, lightless, reinforced closet deep in the depths of the ship, where the shrieking of the ship's timbers joined the skittering of the rats.

To make their imprisonment complete, Abeke and Meilin were chained together at the ankles with heavy links of iron.

"Voices," Abeke whispered urgently. "Someone's coming. Get up!"

Meilin eased gracefully to her feet, managing to stay noiseless even with the heavy chain linking her ankle to Abeke's. She might be shackled and broken, but she still had the reflexes of a warrior.

The candlelight that leaked in would have been dim in any other circumstance, but after days in near darkness, Abeke was dazzled. Once her eyes adjusted, she saw a boy in the doorway. He was tall and well built, with pale skin and soft, apologetic eyes. Shane.

Though she held no love for any of the Conquerors, Abeke knew Shane was the closest they had to an ally. Throughout their long boat journey, he'd been the only one to bring them food to eat and fresh water to drink. They'd have died without him.

Abeke could sense the fury coming off Meilin in waves, but her friend held silent. This was Abeke's relationship to navigate.

"Are you two okay?" Shane asked. His tone was gentle, but Abeke was well aware of the saber glinting at the boy's waist, of the power Shane had over them. He was still one of their captors. And Shane was capable of summoning his own ferocious spirit animal, a wolverine. Abeke was confident her leopard, Uraza, could best the creature in normal circumstances, but wolverines were perfectly suited to fighting in close quarters, and Uraza was not.

"We're as good as can be expected," Abeke said curtly, conspicuously rattling their chain.

"I'm truly sorry about that," Shane said, sighing. "I told them there was no need for shackles." He broke off, staring at the ceiling. Scraping sounds came from above. "Your time in the hold is over, anyway. We've arrived at our stronghold."

Abeke narrowed her eyes. Was he expecting her to be relieved? She had no fondness for the brig, but knew that whatever awaited in the Conqueror base was worse. Were they planning to sacrifice Abeke and Meilin to Gerathon, the Great Serpent? Or force Abeke to drink the awful Bile, so she'd be a puppet the Great Beast could control at will, like Meilin?

Abeke struggled to keep her composure, but when she thought of that day at Mulop's grotto, frightening images passed through her mind: Meilin's fingers tight on her arm, digging to the bone as she cruelly hauled her down to the rocky beach. Fighting to get free, only to see Meilin's quarterstaff come smashing down hard against her skull. The world fading from view. . . .

"*Our* stronghold?" Abeke said, swallowing back the memory. "Whose was it before the Conquerors took it over?"

"It's a palace of one of the lords of the Niloan steppes," Shane said with another sigh. "Listen, I'm not proud that we've taken over someone's home. The lord is still alive, and I'm doing my best to make sure the Niloans who work and live here are kept safe and have enough to eat. I'm trying to make the best of this situation."

Abeke crossed her arms and frowned at him.

"Please come easily with me now, Abeke," Shane said, eyes downcast. "For your sake, and Meilin's."

Abeke glanced at Meilin, who nodded imperceptibly. If Shane was the closest they had to an ally, best to keep him on their side while they got as much information as they could.

"Yes," Abeke said. "We'll submit, Shane. Lead the way."

The ship's ladder was difficult to navigate with chained ankles. Abeke went up a rung, waited until Meilin was right behind her, then took another step. Finally they broke outside. It was overcast, at least, but still the light was blinding. The moment she hit daylight Abeke had to scrunch her eyes shut, tears streaming down her face.

Shane was there waiting, and with strong hands pulled Abeke and Meilin from the last rung so they were sitting on the deck.

Only slowly did Abeke's eyes adjust. The moment they did, she gasped.

On deck was a score of Conquerors, loading up a skiff to head to shore. The soldiers wore a uniform of simple leather armor, with breastplates rubbed black with oil. This armor wasn't ceremonial. It was made for unencumbered fighting.

It's for fighting Niloans, Abeke thought bitterly. *Fighting people who are defending their homes.*

Zerif was there, not a foot away, the man who had once tricked Abeke into thinking she was joining the side of good. He still had the same handsome, severely lined face and tight-cropped beard. Beside him was a slender woman

Abeke hadn't seen since her time in the North: Aidana, Rollan's mother. Though she was unchained, she looked a bit like a prisoner herself, with a gaunt face and exhausted eyes. For the first time, Abeke was relieved that Rollan wasn't near; seeing his mother in such a wretched state might have destroyed him.

That wasn't all, though. Next to Aidana was a girl Abeke didn't recognize. She was tall and pale, with large eyes and a sly, curving smile. The girl wore a suit of black leather, banded with strips of ivory carved to look like spider legs. She cut her gaze to Abeke and Meilin, then to Shane, her lips barely moving as she spoke. "*These* are the moths you've worked so hard to net, brother? I'm disappointed."

Brother! Abeke took in the girl's sharp jaw, her high cheekbones and thick white-blond hair, and saw the resemblance. This girl was one of the Marked too; a spider, as large as a seagull, was perched on her shoulder. Banded in yellow, its swollen abdomen declared that it was venomous.

For a moment Shane seemed taken aback by his sister's words, but when he spoke his voice was mocking. "Drina. Want to tell us again about your many times losing to the Keeper of Greenhaven? Or would you prefer not to talk about it?"

Shane had drawn blood. Now it was Drina's turn to look wounded, though when she noticed Zerif watching her face hardened, turned scoffing. Abeke sensed that this conversation between siblings would have gone differently if Zerif hadn't been there.

"Enough!" Zerif barked, right as Drina opened her mouth to retort. "Victory in Nilo is almost at hand – there is no need to squabble like children."

Abeke risked a glance at Meilin – dissension among the Conquerors might be something that they could use to their advantage. But Meilin sat still on the deck, palms open on her knees, eyes shut. Taking in nothing.

The four Conquerors – Shane, Zerif, Aidana, and Drina – stared down at Abeke and Meilin. As they did, the sun emerged from behind its clouds, and in the sudden light Abeke couldn't make out their faces. They were just four figures cut out of the sky, looming over the chained girls. She felt wretched to be so helpless before them.

"Not much to look at, are they?" Zerif asked. "But then, I knew from the moment I met Abeke that we had nothing to fear from her. Even her father seemed disappointed in the girl. He must be even more disappointed now, with Okaihee in the middle of conquered territory."

A familiar feeling of powerless rage swelled in Abeke. It was like back in her village, when her sister, Soama, would hold Abeke's hair from her face and catalog her flaws. What Soama had most wanted was to feel pretty, and the easiest way to accomplish that had been to make Abeke feel ugly. She'd learned to keep her face perfectly still then, and she tried to do that again now. All the same, she yearned to release Uraza and see the leopard lock her fangs around Zerif's throat. But the Conqueror had his jackal spirit animal threading between his ankles. The beast had alert eyes, and it revealed sharp teeth as it panted. Drina's spider was up high on her shoulder, crouching, as if to pounce. It would be foolish to attack.

"On your feet," Zerif ordered.

Abeke hesitated, but Meilin dragged herself up, chains clanking. Abeke looked at her friend's face and found it blank. For a moment, she worried that Meilin wasn't Meilin, that she'd been possessed by Gerathon. But then Abeke saw that Meilin's fists were clenched.

"Now," Zerif said, smiling cruelly. He crossed his arms. "Get back onto your knees."

Abeke glanced at Shane, who seemed at a loss in the face of the man's sadism. Meilin quivered with barely repressed rage. *Don't attack*, Abeke mentally pleaded. *Now isn't the time.*

"He said *on your knees*!" Drina kicked her foot out. She was quick, much more so than Abeke would have anticipated. It was like the girl had the very same reflexes as her spider. Before she knew what was happening, Abeke and Meilin were on their knees. Abeke's chin hit the deck hard, and she tasted blood in her mouth.

"Drina!" she heard Shane say. "Stop it."

Abeke kept her eyes closed in the long moment that followed. She was surprised to hear how repentant Drina's voice sounded when she spoke again. "I'm sorry, brother."

Zerif chortled. "Gar wants them brought ashore, but dear me if he didn't say *how*. When we last met, Abeke tried to fire an arrow through my heart. It's my right to exact payment. I say they swim."

Shane started to protest, but the words were lost. Abeke felt a heavy boot at her back, and then she was rolling forward across the deck. For a moment she was stopped by the chain that linked her to Meilin. Then she heard a whump and a cry as Zerif kicked Meilin too. Abeke heard her friend skid across the deck, and then she was falling.

Overboard.

Abeke clawed at the deck's planks, desperately trying to get a handhold, but all she got were fistfuls of splinters. She could hear Meilin's cries from over the side of the ship, her weight dragging Abeke over. Shane's shocked face was the last thing she saw as she whipped over the deck and through open air. She heard Meilin splash, and then impacted the water a moment later.

Abeke's stomach plummeted, and the shock of cold salt water ripped at her mouth. The heavy chain was dragging them into the depths. Abeke swam against it on impulse, stroking toward the surface. It was nearly impossible to make any headway; only by pulling at the water with all her might could she stop from sinking farther. Meilin foundered somewhere below, dragging Abeke down.

Finally the pull on the chain lessened, and Abeke was able to break into open air. She slapped frantically at the water to prevent being pulled back under. Through stinging eyes she saw that Meilin was beside her, fighting just as hard to stay above the surface. Abeke's muscles were already on fire. They would only be able to keep this up for moments before they'd succumb and sink.

Meilin was gasping, and the chain got heavier and heavier. Abeke couldn't spare the energy to look up, but she distantly heard Shane's voice calling for help. Drina was shouting at Zerif, and even she sounded panicked.

Shane yelled down. "Abeke, swim to shore! Swim to shore! It's not far."

Desperate, Abeke searched for the shoreline. Shane was wrong. Between the drag of the chain and the searing of her salt-scoured lungs, the shore looked impossibly far away. But it was their only hope.

"Meilin!" she cried. "This might be our chance! Come on!"

Amid Drina's screeching and Shane's bellowing, Abeke began to swim. It felt like someone had set fires in her exhausted legs. Meilin was beside her, at least, matching Abeke's crawling pace through the water. The Zhongese girl, too, was screaming with the exertion. "Come on, Meilin!" Abeke urged as she swam. "We can do this!"

Despite her determination, Abeke's arms began to slow. Her legs submitted to the merciless chain, sinking lower and lower in the water, and salt water dribbled into her mouth with every gasping breath. She felt Meilin's hands under her arms, trying to help keep her afloat, but it was too late. Abeke was foundering, the water closing tight over her head.

And then her feet touched ground.

A sandbar!

Meilin got to her feet beside Abeke and laughed with relief. Seawater might have been up to their throats, but they weren't drowning anymore. For a long minute both girls panted and recovered.

Meilin glanced back at the ship. "Zerif is insane," she said. "The Conquerors clearly want us alive, or they would have killed us back in Oceanus. So why would he risk drowning us?"

"I nearly killed him," Abeke said, distracted. "I guess that can make someone testy. But for now we have other things to worry about. Meilin, look!"

At the shore, the sea itself was walking. In front of them, the surf split into two as a huge shape planed through the water. At first Abeke imagined that an undersea boulder was rolling with the tide. But then she saw, beneath the wave, a thrashing tail covered with leather plates. A giant crocodile came to a stop in the surf not a dozen yards away. It stared at the two exhausted girls.

A tall armored figure waded in from the shoreline, a horned mask covering his face. He approached the crocodile and laid a hand on its snout. The man crossed his heavily muscled arms and stared at Abeke and Meilin, trapped on the sandbar.

General Gar, the leader of the Conquerors, was waiting for them. The Devourer.

2

OKAIHEE

ROLLAN KNEW MAKING THEIR WAY ACROSS NILO TO FIND the Golden Lion of Cabaro would mean struggling to survive in hostile territory, but he'd consoled himself that at least it would be hot, like the Concorba of his early years. During the day they all sweated plenty – Rollan's tunic was still ringed in salt stains. But now that the sun had gone down, he was shivering. Rollan was glad for the spot where his shoulder touched Conor's. It felt like the only part of his body that was warm.

The evening was pretty, Rollan would give it that. The stars were thick in the sky, occasionally blotted by the silhouettes of slender trees swaying in the breeze. Tarik had stopped them on a sandy bluff overlooking a small village, where they were just barely camouflaged by a scrawny, scaly bush. *Okaihee might be occupied by Conquerors*, Tarik had warned. *We should watch for a while to see who goes in and out.*

So far, that meant precisely no one. As the evening wrapped them in its chill, the ruddy cooking fires on the other side of the palisade were starting to look very attractive to Rollan. Even if those fires turned out to be surrounded by the enemy, at least they would be warm.

Chances were that Okaihee *was* occupied – in all the villages they'd come to so far, the chiefs had either been killed or had pledged support to the Conquerors in return for protection. Tarik had explained that what "protection" really meant was their children wouldn't be pressed into service, and only half their crops would be seized to feed the invading armies.

Though Okaihee looked calm, they'd learned the hard way to move cautiously into villages. The day before they'd approached a village chief, only to be surrounded by a half dozen Conquerors before they knew it, one of whom fought alongside a particularly vicious lynx. Rollan ran his fingers over the bandaged wound on his forearm. Meilin would have pretended to be repulsed by the scar, but Rollan thought she'd be secretly impressed.

Meilin. Where was she?

If only he knew. Their campaign in Oceanus had ended in such a whirlwind. They'd finally met Mulop the Octopus, who gave up his Coral Octopus willingly, cautioning them why the Devourer was so intent on collecting the talismans guarded by the Great Beasts – he was going to free Kovo the Ape from his prison.

But that's when things went really bad. Rollan was haunted by the strange, sick look in Meilin's eyes when she'd turned on them. Even worse was that he'd recognized it from his mother, Aidana, when *she* had been controlled by Gerathon. Twice now he had nearly been killed by people he cared about and forced to stare down the Great Serpent through their eyes.

Rollan shook his head, trying to get his thoughts back on the Okaihee palisade. But the vision of possessed Meilin, her face impassive as she dragged Abeke toward the Conquerors, kept returning to his mind. It was like the universe was trying to prove something to him: *You will be left time and again. Loving you is a curse.*

Whenever Rollan saw Essix's outline pass before the scant moonlit clouds in the night sky, his suffering slackened. At least the falcon had been faithful – and was starting to act as if she almost liked him. If it hadn't been for her, he might not have been able to go forward with their mission. Tarik too: The elder Greencloak had been rock-steady as he led them deeper and deeper into the occupied lands of Nilo, though Rollan knew that the loss of Meilin and Abeke had affected him. Maybe more than he could afford to show.

"Hey, Rollan," Conor said. Rollan startled at the voice. His best friend, with his calm and trusting eyes, looked concerned by what he found in Rollan's expression. "Are you okay?"

"Yes," Rollan said. He shifted on the ground. "Well, you know, I'm freezing. And there's sand in my underpants. And a thorn is literally in my side. But otherwise, I'm doing great."

"You just . . ." Conor said, his voice trailing off. He coughed. "I was thinking, just for myself, that it's important that we talk about what happened as much as we can."

"You can't be serious," Rollan said. "We're in occupied

territory, trying to track down one of the last free talismans, and you're worried about our *feelings*?"

Tarik, on his belly on the far side of Conor, reached across the boy to lay a hand on Rollan's shoulder. He whispered, "What you mean to say is that you agree with Conor. That we should keep reminding ourselves that it wasn't Meilin's fault. It wasn't, and it isn't. And we'll find her and Abeke. But it's okay to feel upset about it. It breaks me apart that they were taken. But all the same, we can't pretend they weren't."

"For the love of Mulop!" Rollan said. "*Both* of you?! I can't believe what I'm hearing. Tarik, I expected better."

Tarik clamped his strong hand over Rollan's mouth.

"Hmph," Rollan said, straining to lift the man's fingers. "Mmph!"

"Shh," whispered the senior Greencloak, returning to his survey of the village.

"Yeah!" Conor joined. "*Shh*, Rollan."

Tarik clamped his other hand over Conor's mouth. "There's something moving out there. On the far right side of the palisade. I can't quite tell. Rollan, could you –"

"On it," Rollan said. Or "hmphit," since Tarik's hand was still over his mouth. As Tarik lifted it, Rollan let his consciousness drift to Essix, who was circling the palisade, high in the air currents above.

This was a trick Rollan had picked up while they were battling through Nilo. One day his mind had been wandering, and he peered up at the falcon and thought to himself: *What would it be like to see the savannah from up there?* Then, ominously, his vision blacked out. After a sick moment of panic, he'd seen a pinprick of light appear at the center of the blackness, and suddenly Rollan could see again.

That's when he really panicked.

Because what Rollan had seen was the world from a thousand feet up. He was looking *through* Essix's eyes. Somehow she'd snatched up his daydreaming mind like a delicious desert mouse and carried it soaring over the savannah. It took a few more tries before he finally stopped screaming and learned to enjoy it.

The falcon's eyes were on either side of her head, and the first sensation Rollan had now was of how wide open the world was. He could see above, below, and on both sides, simultaneously taking in the yellow moon, the forests to the north, the swamps to the west, and the motion of a flying squirrel as it leaped between tree branches. The falcon's vision never stayed in one place for more than a moment, ever flitting among the grasses and buildings below. Essix was obviously used to the way her eyes worked, but it made Rollan feel like he was tumbling down a hill with his eyes open. His stomach clenched at the constant motion. Still, something caught his attention. Something big.

"There's an elephant," he reported. His vision was still with Essix, but he'd learned he could speak through his own mouth if he concentrated. "Pressing against the palisade wall."

"An elephant? Like Dinesh?" Conor asked, Briggan rumbling worriedly in the background.

"Much smaller than Dinesh – this is a normal elephant. But yes."

Essix cried in the night and flew tighter circles over the elephant at the palisade. "It's . . . breaking down the wall, like it's trying to bash its way through," Rollan reported. "Something has it spooked."

Conor grunted. "Are there any Conquerors with it?"

"No," Rollan said, returning to his own vision to see Conor searching the shadows. "It's alone."

Conor opened his mouth, but then stilled when they heard a tremendous crash.

"Hold on," Rollan said. "Let me get back into Essix's vision."

"No need," Tarik said, squinting into the darkness. He crouched on his feet, curved sword at the ready, his powerful body tensed. "It's quite clear what happened. That elephant knocked down the palisade wall. It is probably a Bile-fed puppet of the Conquerors. Okaihee has been breached."

"Come on," Conor said to Briggan. The wolf had been dozing only a minute ago, head heavy on his paws. But now he was on his feet, growling softly. "It's time to go help Okaihee."

"Don't you think," Rollan said, "that maybe we should *avoid* the insane elephant?"

Conor, Tarik, and even Briggan stared back at him balefully. "Okay," Rollan said, getting to his feet. "Fine, let's go. I was starting to get termites up my pant legs anyway."

As they stole down the hillside toward the noise, shouts rose from the village as the elephant progressed through Okaihee.

When they reached the palisade, they saw that the wall had been trampled. Logs and rope were jumbled along either side. They heard another large crash from the far side of Okaihee, and Briggan crouched, growling.

"It seems our elephant found its own way out," Rollan said.

"Well," Tarik said. "If Abeke's village *has* been occupied by the Conquerors, this would be a good distraction to use to our advantage. We should find Chinwe as soon as possible. She's a faithful Greencloak, and was present at Abeke's Nectar Ceremony. She can help fill us in on what's happening here, and might be able to point us toward the Golden Lion of Cabaro."

They started forward, but Tarik raised a hand to stop them. "Above all, be alert to Conquerors. I don't want to lose you two, as well."

Rollan sensed Essix gliding over them as they crept into the village. Briggan loomed large in the moonlight, but Rollan wasn't too worried the wolf would get them spotted – there weren't signs of Conquerors. In fact, the whole village was eerily quiet. Whoever was shouting earlier must have either chased after the elephant or returned home. All was silent and dark, grass curtains fluttering in the night breezes.

As they crept forward, Rollan in the lead, he couldn't shake the suspicion that they were being watched. He peered into the homes they passed, but could see no one. He approached the fire pit, where the elephant must have finally managed to disentangle itself from the fence debris. Bits of wood and cord were everywhere. Rollan picked at a loose plank with his foot, half-expecting something to lunge out at him. "Conor," he finally said, "do you sense any –"

Suddenly Rollan was on his back, a sharpened stick jabbing into his throat. He batted it away on reflex, but then the point was back, pressing right into his windpipe. "Help!" Rollan managed to cry, the sound strangled by the thrusting weapon. Then he saw who was assaulting him.

It was a skinny girl, a bit younger than himself.

Rollan could see Tarik and Conor creeping behind the girl, both crouched low to the ground, ready to pounce if she made a wrong move. Beside Conor, Briggan growled, a noise that sent the hairs on Rollan's arms on end – and that was knowing the wolf was on *his* side.

But the girl didn't seem afraid. As she stared into his eyes, Rollan saw a dullness to her gaze, a sense of what-more-could-life-do-to-me? He recognized it from the street orphans he'd known in Concorba. This girl had been through trauma.

"We're not here to hurt you," Tarik said from behind her. "You don't need to threaten him."

The girl stared down at Rollan flatly, ignoring Tarik.

Rollan wanted to speak, but the stick was still jammed firmly into his neck. All he could do was continue to stare up at his attacker, his eyes wide.

"We're friends of Abeke," Tarik continued. "She used to live in this village. Do you know her?"

The girl's eyes lit slightly. She turned her head, and the pressure on the stick at Rollan's throat lessened.

"Can you tell us where Chinwe is? We'd like to speak to her."

The girl's eyes cast back down.

"What's your name?" Rollan croaked, rubbing his throat.

"Irtike," the girl mumbled.

"Irtike," Rollan said. "Can you tell us where Chinwe is?"

"She's dead," the girl whispered simply. Finally she stepped away from Rollan and stood at ease, though still gripping her sharpened stick. "She was killed by the Conquerors while protecting Okaihee during the first invasion. We gave her a funeral at the end of the last rainy season."

Tarik bowed his head. "You have my sympathies. She was a strong, kind woman. The village must be mourning her loss very much."

"Is Okaihee under Conqueror control now?" Rollan asked, crawling to his feet.

"No," the girl whispered. "Abeke's father, Pojalo, became the new chieftain when our old one was killed defending the village, with Chinwe. He has worked hard ever since to keep us beneath the Conquerors' notice. They leave us alone because there is little of value left here. Our crops have all failed."

"Where is Pojalo?" Tarik asked.

Irtike pointed to a hut indistinguishable from the rest, at the other side of the fire pit.

"Thank you," Rollan said. He felt her stare hot on his back as he turned to confer with his companions.

Tarik shook his head grimly. "Chinwe was a capable and courageous fighter, with a powerful wildebeest at her side. If anyone could have led us safely to Cabaro, it was her. If even she has fallen . . ."

"We'll find a way," Conor said. "You're the best fighter the Greencloaks have."

"I'm glad for your confidence," Tarik said, a weak smile on his face. "But I'd hoped to find allies here. With Meilin and Abeke gone, and Chinwe dead . . . We've lost so many great warriors. So many friends."

After a moment, Tarik seemed to find some inner reservoir of courage. He lifted his head resolutely and led them toward Pojalo's hut. Rollan heard a rush of wind and felt Essix's familiar talons on his shoulder. He stroked the bird's clawed leg. She surprised him by giving an affectionate nip in response.

"It's the custom in this region that a visitor be introduced to the chief by another member of the village," Tarik said. "It's a wise practice, since it gets the community invested in one another's affairs and prevents outsiders from manipulating any one villager. But I don't know how we'll get an introduction to the chief, with Chinwe gone."

Something sharp jabbed Rollan in the back and he jumped. "Aiee! Hey!"

When Rollan whirled, he saw a small figure with now-familiar solemn eyes blinking up at him.

"I'll introduce you," Irtike declared. She swept her braids back from her thin face and smoothed her simple wrap over her narrow hips.

Conor chuckled. "Looks like you've made a new friend."

Rollan glared at Conor. He opened his mouth to speak, had so many things he wanted to say about girls who snuck up on people and jabbed them with spears.

"Thank you, Irtike," Tarik said, intervening. "We are honored."

Irtike nodded, then loped gracefully to the chief's doorway. She called something in the local language, then listened for a response. After a male voice shouted back, Irtike pulled aside the heavy grass curtain and ushered them inside.

The hut, so unassuming from the outside, was actually very spacious. A cooking pit was at the center, an iron pot steaming away over hot embers, giving off a wonderful aroma of greens and cream and nuts. Banded chests were stacked at one side, and at the other was a long table set for a simple meal. At the far end of the hut was a man Rollan assumed was the new chieftain, Abeke's father, Pojalo. He wore a length of beaded red fabric wrapped around his head. Beside him was a girl who was unmistakably Abeke's sister.

Abeke had once said Soama was the more beautiful sister, but that's not how Rollan would have put it. Lips lined with kohl, a beaded headpiece flashing on her forehead, the girl simply looked more . . . precious than Abeke. It wasn't a quality Rollan particularly admired.

Irtike whispered to Pojalo, and he nodded gravely in return, the scowl on his face not lifting. When he gestured to a low wicker stool at his side, Irtike shyly ducked her head and sat on it.

"Greetings," Tarik said. "We are–"

Soama made a tsk, and Tarik fell silent. They all stared at one another. *Awkward*, thought Rollan, while Irtike stared furiously into the ground. Taking a cue from her, Rollan began scrutinizing the dusty wicker mat below his feet.

Pojalo finally spoke. "You may state your business now."

"I am Tarik, and these young warriors are Conor and Rollan. We are Greencloaks, and come with tidings of your daughter. Abeke –"

"And those are the Great Beasts Briggan and Essix," Pojalo interrupted. "My daughter summoned a Great Beast too. Uraza the Leopard."

"She certainly did," Tarik said, a strained smile on his face. "And it ushered in an extraordinary time. Actually," he continued, "I would like to speak to you about your daughter."

But Pojalo raised a finger to stop him. "When my daughter summoned Uraza," he said, "it marked her as special. Our tribe has been without a Rain Dancer for years, and we had hopes that Abeke would serve as our next. But she was taken by the Greencloaks. By you."

"Excuse me," Rollan said. Even though he wasn't a Greencloak, himself – no way was he going to spend his whole life obeying someone else's orders – Rollan was irked that Pojalo had gotten it so wrong. Abeke had *not* been taken by the Greencloaks. It had been Zerif, masquerading as a Greencloak.

Rollan was about to say so when Pojalo held up a hand to silence him. It only made Rollan want to talk louder, of course, but then he saw Irtike make an almost unnoticeable "back off" gesture with her fingers. Remembering the sharp stick she'd pressed so confidently to his jugular, Rollan obeyed her.

"If we'd had a Rain Dancer, we would have had rain," Pojalo said. "But you Greencloaks took Abeke from us, and so our drought continues. Our crops have failed. We were famished and weak when the Conquerors attacked, and we soon lost our previous chief, as well as our Greencloak, Chinwe. If you are as concerned as you claim about the Conquerors dominating Nilo, perhaps you should not have taken the one person who might have kept us strong. We are a proud people, but it's only a matter of time until we will have to submit, like so many others. I will keep Okaihee independent as long as I can. But if you hope to save Nilo, then all I can say is that you have gone about it foolishly so far."

Why hadn't Pojalo asked about Abeke yet? Rollan opened his mouth to speak, but Conor beat him to the question. "Perhaps, my lord, you would like to hear of your daughter?" he asked.

Pojalo glared at Conor. "You use polite titles, boy, but in Nilo it is the chieftain who decides who will speak when."

Rollan had seen Conor scolded by nobility before. Back in Trunswick, the young lord Devin had once silenced him with a similar tone, and Rollan had watched his meek, gentle friend recoil from the rebuke, his face full of shame. But a lot had changed since Trunswick. Now, Conor's face flushed with anger and his eyes glinted. Even Briggan's hackles were raised.

"*You* have permission to speak," the chieftain said, gesturing to Tarik.

"We bear news of Abeke, when you wish to hear it," Tarik said, speaking carefully. "But right now, you should know that we witnessed an elephant break the village's palisade. Surely you heard the noise."

Soama and her father exchanged a look. "This is not the first time we have experienced such a disturbance," Pojalo said. "But there are few able adults left in Okaihee, and I cannot rally them until morning. We must hope that the Conquerors will not take advantage of the breach before we can repair it."

"I fear," Tarik said, "that the elephant could be here precisely as part of a plan to attack your village. Wherever there are Conquerors, there are also animals who have been force-fed Bile and turned into monsters. Perhaps this elephant is their puppet. It seems likely that it broke the palisade precisely so the enemy force could enter after it."

Pojalo chuckled. "Oh yes, that elephant was indeed being controlled. But not by the Conquerors. You know less of the current situation in Nilo than you think, stranger."

Rollan couldn't resist speaking up. "What do you mean?"

Pojalo sighed in frustration, pinching the bridge of his nose. "I suppose it couldn't hurt to tell you. We have had . . . numerous animals entering our village lately. They always arrive from the north and leave toward the south. Any wild creature that was thinking straight would go around, but they are single-minded in their path. We cleared out the huts from the center of the village so they could have an unobstructed course and do less damage. The Conquerors are a bad enough problem, but that elephant was not sent by them. It was not possessed by Bile."

"Who, then, is behind this strange animal behavior?" Tarik asked.

Pojalo hung his head. It was Soama who spoke, her voice both proud and faint, like she'd once had much poise but had been brought low by recent times. "They say he was the first creature to settle in Nilo, that he has been here for eons, since long before the age of man. He is as old as the savannah itself. A mighty titan, a giant lion who lives in a secluded oasis in the southern desert. He hates all humans." The girl's voice dropped low. "Cabaro the Lion."

"The Great Beast," Conor mouthed.

"It is Cabaro that we search for!" Tarik said. "We need to secure his talisman before the Conquerors can get it first. We've recently learned that they mean to use the talismans to free Kovo the Ape from his prison. If they succeed, then whatever hope we have of resisting the Conquerors will be dashed."

"Interesting," Pojalo said, leaning forward as he weighed the words in his mouth. "What do you intend?"

"Our passage through Nilo has been difficult, and we have already lost precious allies. We need your aid to get farther, and someone who can help us negotiate with the tribes that we pass. We need someone who knows this terrain. We were hoping Chinwe could come with us–"

"Chinwe is dead."

Tarik nodded gravely. "Irtike has told us as much. We are sorry for the loss–yours and ours."

Pojalo cut Irtike a harsh look. "You spoke to them? You didn't bring them directly to me?"

"Oh, believe me," Rollan said. "She didn't exactly greet us with hugs and kisses."

Irtike spoke, her voice quiet but her jaw jutting out defiantly. "I intervened only to tell them about my mother."

Chinwe was Irtike's mother! No wonder she had that numbed-over look that Rollan recognized from his fellow orphans in Concorba.

"Do you think," Tarik said, "that you might be able to spare some able bodies? Our goals are aligned, after all; you must want to see the Conquerors defeated as much as we do."

Rollan looked hopefully to Soama. But the girl had her arms clamped across her chest, her otherwise beautiful face twisted into a scowl.

Pojalo shook his head. "No, our goals are not aligned. Between the droughts and the turmoil in Nilo, I have lost most of the 'able bodies' that Okaihee had. It is only because there is nothing of value left here that the Conquerors have lately directed their energies elsewhere in the region. If they hear I have helped you, they will return and attack. We cannot survive another assault."

"Please," Tarik said. "This is about the fate of all Erdas. If the Conquerors get their hands on the Golden Lion of Cabaro, I can assure you that will also mean the end of Okaihee."

"My daughter once wrote similar words to me, pleading about the fate of Erdas!" Pojalo yelled, suddenly on his feet. "That was when she told me she was not coming back. You have taken too much already. I won't sacrifice anything else to the Greencloaks."

Tarik looked as if he'd been struck. In the days since Meilin and Abeke were captured, the Greencloak guardian had stood a little less tall, walked a little less surely–as if he carried a burden that grew heavier with each passing day. Rollan had shrugged it off before. They were all fatigued, after all. But now, for the first time, Tarik appeared to be at a loss.

The thought scared Rollan.

"You don't even care about what happened to Abeke," Conor said. His voice was calm and controlled, but his eyes had narrowed. Beside him, Briggan growled. Not much of a game face, that wolf.

For a moment the hut was still, tension thick in the air. Irtike's eyes flitted from Conor to Pojalo and back again.

Finally the chieftain spoke, straightening to his full regal bearing. "I do not. Abeke is dead to me. And do not disrespect me by speaking out of turn again. I will not stand for it."

"She is the pride of the Greencloaks!" Conor cried. "She's saved countless lives. You should be *proud* of your daughter."

"Stop!" Pojalo barked, tears in his eyes. "I do not wish to hear of this!"

"Ow!" Rollan shouted, louder than either of them. All attention in the hut turned to him. Essix had pierced his shoulder with her talons. He rubbed the wound. "What was *that* for?"

Then he followed Essix's gaze to the entrance of the hut and staggered to his feet.

A lion had slinked in, head bobbing close to the ground as it sniffed the air. Rollan had seen a pride of lions from afar while they were trekking through the savannah, but this was the first time he had seen one up close.

This particular specimen was lean, almost scrawny, its rib bones visible under its skin and its mane sticking out in irregular tufts. The lion took all of them in, then returned to searching the ground, sniffing. It took a step toward the fire pit in the center, but recoiled from the heat and stepped toward the far wall.

They were all on their feet now, weapons drawn. Rollan glanced at Conor and Tarik, trying to determine if they planned to attack. The lion was, well, a *lion*. But it wasn't aggressive; it was just trying to pass south through the hut, and in its single-minded state hadn't realized there wasn't a second exit.

The lion seemed to have discovered it was trapped. It raised its head and flattened its ears. Displaying its teeth, it let out an angry yowl.

Rollan swallowed. Those teeth were very long.

"The lion's not attacking. Back off from it!" Tarik shouted.

The Greencloak was pressed against the wall but had his curved sword at the ready. He clearly had the same idea that Rollan did: best to give the lost animal a chance to leave on its own.

But that lion, so near, was apparently too much for Soama to take. The girl sprinted for the doorway.

Immediately Rollan realized her error – the lion was penned in now, with no way to escape. It roared, the sound loud enough to make Soama scream out and Irtike drop to her knees. The cat charged Soama, who had gone limp in fear.

Next thing Rollan knew, Essix's fierce wingbeats were buffeting his head. The falcon was on the lion, talons sinking into the animal's backside. Rollan had thought it looked scrawny for a giant cat, but it was clearly extremely strong. The lion jumped into the air and twisted, its whole spine rotating. The motion of it catapulted Essix off, and the falcon hit the far wall before she could right herself, sliding to the ground. With impossible grace, the cat landed back on its feet and stalked toward Soama.

Now it was Briggan's turn. The large wolf faced off against the lion, forelegs splayed so his head was low, flesh pulled back from his long teeth as he growled. Yowling in desperation, the lion slapped the air with its paw, claws extended.

Within a moment, the animals were on each other, tumbling in flashes of yellow and gray fur, jaws snapping in open air as they tried to reach each other's throats. Rollan was relieved to see Essix take back to the air while Conor rushed to Briggan's side, brandishing his wooden shepherd's staff. Conor swung it in a wide arc, slamming the lion in the side of its head. The cat fell away from Briggan, rolling in the soil but soon recovering its feet.

It tensed its rear legs, like a crossbow being cocked.

Rollan opened his mouth to warn his friend, but it was too late. The lion launched itself at Conor.

The big cat whooshed through the air. Conor was too stunned to do anything but stumble backward, hands helplessly shielding his face. But Briggan wouldn't let the lion near. He leaped, impacting the cat in midair. When they landed, the wolf's jaw was clamped on the lion's shoulders. It yowled and thrashed, Briggan struggling to keep his feet. Tarik advanced, his curved sword extended, while Rollan took a position at the lion's flank.

Tarik brought his curved sword up. He surprised Rollan by pointing it, not at the lion, but at Soama. "Get out of the entranceway," he bellowed. "Now!"

When Tarik yelled at her, Soama seemed to realize herself. She skirted the hut, keeping her eyes fixed on the lion until she'd reached her father and Irtike. Pojalo shielded his daughter with his body.

The lion struggled to get out from under Briggan's jaws. Rollan realized that the wolf was just holding it by the nape, like an errant puppy; the lion wasn't even bleeding. When Briggan experimentally loosened his grip, the lion bounded free. Hissing, the cat staggered to the exit and limped out of sight.

For a few seconds, all anyone could do was stand in a circle and breathe at one another.

Then Pojalo spoke: "I need to repair my palisade."

"What?" Rollan muttered under his breath, "no thank-you gift?"

"We can help you," Tarik said, pointedly raising his voice so it covered Rollan's. "We should all go now and rig something to secure the village from attack."

"I do not want your help," Pojalo said. "What I want is for you to leave."

Tarik shook his head in resignation. "You're making a mistake. But we will respect your wishes."

Rollan was only half listening. He had Essix in his arms, inspecting her wing bones and feathers for damage. She seemed fine, but was clearly enjoying the preening, making quiet little screeches. Only recently had the falcon seemed to appreciate being groomed and touched by him. First letting Rollan see through her eyes, and now this. Perhaps everyone was changing.

In fact, it was *Conor* who began yelling at the chieftain. Conor!

The boy positioned himself in front of Pojalo, whipping his green cloak behind him in indignation. "I'm not leaving until I say what I came here to say. I stood by and watched while you denied us the help we asked. I stayed silent while you made the wrong choice for your people. But we just fought off a lion to save you, and I will not let you push us out of here before I tell you what happened to Abeke!" He paused. "Sir!"

Pojalo's and Soama's faces went stony. Tarik placed an arm around Conor's shoulder, but Rollan realized with surprise that it was a gesture of support, rather than disapproval.

Conor's face turned pleading. "Your daughter's been captured by the Conquerors. We don't know if she's alive or dead. Please, tell us you care about her, so if we see her again, I can tell her that her father loves her."

"It is clear to me that you will do whatever you want," Pojalo said curtly. "And you will tell Abeke whatever you want to tell her. I do not need to go about explaining myself to you, and I don't need to send coddling words to my daughter. She's made her choices."

Conor appeared stricken. The defiant gleam in his eye was replaced by something else, a look not dissimilar to the dull grief that Irtike wore. Rollan wondered if it had ever occurred to his friend that some parents might not love their children. He hadn't grown up seeing what Rollan had.

"Then there's no point in speaking further," Conor muttered, the fight draining from his voice. "He's right – we should leave."

Briggan growled approvingly, nuzzling Conor's hand.

They left the hut and went out into the night.

"It's unbelievable," Conor said once they were outside, gazing up at the sky. "How could he not care about his own daughter?"

"He's in pain," Tarik said simply. "And the future of Okaihee looks very grim. It's hard to know what he's thinking in such a state. Whatever it is, he clearly doesn't see a need to explain it to us."

Conor bit back whatever he was about to say next.

Tarik tousled Conor's hair. "I'm proud of you," he said. "Sometimes the most important part of leadership is knowing when to let people have a piece of your mind."

Conor nodded thoughtfully, and for once he didn't blush from the praise.

Leadership? Rollan wondered, rolling his eyes. Tarik never spoke to Rollan about leadership. But then again, Conor was the one wearing the green cloak. Rollan wasn't cut out for that sort of thing. It was trouble enough staying alive and keeping an eye out for all the people who might suddenly betray him, without worrying about setting an example for everyone else.

Rollan rubbed the corner of his own slate gray cloak between thumb and forefinger. He wouldn't be turning it in for a green one anytime soon.

“So what do we do now?” he asked, if only to remind them he was still standing there.

“We learned one valuable piece of information here tonight,” Tarik said. “Animals from across Nilo are on their way south to Cabaro.” Tarik turned to Conor. “What do you think we should do?”

Conor considered it. “Our first priority should be the talisman. If the Conquerors get ahold of that, all of Erdas is lost.”

Tarik nodded grimly.

“Sounds good to me too,” Rollan grumbled. “Not that anyone asked.”

As they crossed to the southern edge of the village, Rollan found his mind drifting again. The lion in Pojalo’s hut had been scrawny and half-starved – but it had held its own against the three of them, not to mention Briggan and Essix.

What would fighting a healthy, full-sized lion be like? What would fighting a *Great Beast*–sized lion be like?

Rollan knew their only choice was to find Cabaro before the Conquerors did. But all the same, he wasn’t so sure that he wanted to. Not so sure at all.

3

SNAKE EYES

Conor couldn't understand why any parent would willingly forsake a child. He knew that, as chieftain, Pojalo had many responsibilities. The welfare of Okaihee was first on his mind. But still . . .

Lost in thought, Conor tripped on a root. Cursing, he massaged his toes for a moment and then continued forward. They were marching through the nighttime savannah, and though there was plenty of moonlight it was hard to distinguish roots from the surrounding ground. Conor took a moment to look up at the bright, scattered stars and center himself, then hustled forward.

Abeke had always talked glowingly about her family. The Soama she'd described was so elegant, her father so wise. Now he'd finally met them, and rather than being impressed, all Conor felt was bitter.

Family had a peculiar hold on people, that was for sure. Conor knew that well, having given up the Iron Boar of Rumfuss to protect his own. All the same, he wished

Abeke were with them now. He'd tell her not to take her father's disinterest personally. She'd become like a sister to him, to all of them, and anyone could see what an extraordinary person she was.

Conor's eyes stung as he thought again of the two voices that were missing from their journey, voices that might have been stilled forever, for all he knew.

He took a moment to look into the night sky and mouth some words. Somewhere, Abeke might be seeing the same stars. *Stay strong, Abeke. Keep Meilin safe. Help her forgive herself.*

"Hey, dreamer boy! Pick up the pace!" Rollan said, stumbling into Conor's back and cuffing him on the shoulder. Conor shook his head and renewed his focus, stealing forward into the night. Up at the front, Briggan was alert. His ears were perked, the better to lead the band. But that didn't mean Conor could allow himself to be anything less than vigilant in the dangerous countryside.

Once Conor had forced his thoughts back to their immediate surroundings, his senses benefitted more fully from his affinity with Briggan. The smells of the ground varied: from the crisp smell of parched grass to the nutty flavors of exposed roots. There were the musky smells of underground creatures and the slightly blander, watery fragrance of a termite mound. Even in the near-blackness, Conor could move quickly between the scents.

Tarik had decided that they would travel only during the nighttime, to maximize their chances of avoiding Conqueror patrols. It meant losing the advantage of sight, however, making Briggan's sense of smell essential to their safety. With Briggan right in front of him, Conor found that his footsteps were surer. Tarik and Rollan followed behind, stepping only where Briggan and Conor did.

They couldn't be more than a few miles south of Okaihee, but already the landscape was changing. The grassy smell began to hit Conor only rarely, replaced by a pungent, acidic fragrance, like aloe. Conor suspected they were approaching the jungle. Briggan must have sensed it too, as he slowed and came to a gradual halt. The wolf was comfortable traveling the grassland at night, but the jungle was something else entirely.

"The landscape is changing," Conor announced, beckoning his friends in near.

"Do you sense any Conquerors around?" Tarik asked, his voice so close Conor could feel his breath on this throat.

Conor sniffed the air – he could smell animals near, but no people. "No," he said.

Tarik lit a torch, and the glow bathed the faces of the three humans, the glittering eyes of the wolf, and the warm and mischievous eyes of Lumeo. The otter was wrapped around the back of Tarik's neck. With a whoosh, Essix appeared out of the night sky and settled on Rollan's shoulder. Conor jumped.

"Don't worry. I'll never get used to that either," Rollan said.

"By my memory of Niloan geography, if we're near the jungle, then we've made good progress toward the talisman," Tarik said. "Cabaro is thought to live in an oasis in the desert south of the jungle."

"*Thought* to?" Rollan asked, raising an eyebrow. Essix tweaked his ear with her beak. "Ow! What was that for?"

"Maybe she wants you to respect your elders," Tarik said dryly.

"Fine," Rollan said, rubbing his ear. "That hurt!"

Essix gave him an affectionate nuzzle while Tarik pivoted with the torch, scanning the area. "I was hoping there'd be someplace nearby where we could hide out during the day. But this stretch of savannah is wide open. We could move forward into the jungle and camp there, but I don't relish that idea."

"It's our best option," Conor said. "We can't safely camp out in the open like this. The Conquerors could spot us the moment dawn broke."

Tarik shook his head. "Leopards hunt the jungle at night, and they won't be friendly like Uraza. If we get eaten by jungle creatures, the Devourer can take his time getting the talismans he needs to free Kovo. We should stop now and find the best shelter we can, or at least some cover."

"But there *is* no cover," Rollan said. He continued grumpily: "I'll sleep wherever you order me to, my dear generals."

Conor shot him a what's-got-you-so-cranky? look. But it wasn't hard to figure out. Abeke was missing . . . and Meilin. They were traveling all night and sleeping fitfully during the day. Conor knew he was grumpy too, somewhere deep inside, but he'd resolved not to let his own bad mood near the surface.

"Briggan and I can scout while you two boil water for our meal," Conor said. "There has to be a stand of trees somewhere around here." Conor didn't love the idea of wandering the dark savannah, even with the aid of wolf senses, but there wasn't much choice. Could Briggan's acute sense of smell pick up a cobra or a black mamba? He wondered what a snake even smelled like.

"Did you hear that?" Rollan hissed, unsheathing his long dagger. Trusting his friend's instincts, Conor loosened the hand ax at his belt. Soon he heard it too – a chattering sound, coming from the north. Heading right for them.

"What is it?" Tarik said. His eyes scanned the dark. Lumeo stood on Tarik's shoulder and arched his back, hackles raised and teeth bared.

The smell was a little musty, with undertones of fruit. "Monkeys," Conor breathed. "I think they're monkeys."

"Lots and lots of monkeys," Rollan said.

"Oh," Tarik said as the first animal appeared at the edge of the torchlight. "Those are baboons. Not usually dangerous. Everyone hold still."

The first baboon, a swollen pregnant female with another infant on her back, passed right between them, ignoring the travelers as fully as if they'd been trees. Then the next baboons came, a pair of juveniles no higher than Conor's knee. One paused for a moment to stare up at him with its pinched brown eyes, before continuing south.

"More animals on a mission," Rollan said. "And heading south, like the rest, if I'm judging the direction right."

Tarik's face went stony as he peered into the torchlight. "Many, *many* animals heading south."

Four baboons soon became ten, then dozens and hundreds. It was a large troop of them, sweeping across the grassland in one unbroken mass. They shrieked loudly, squabbling with one another as they moved.

Then the full horde was suddenly upon them. They were on all sides, so there was nowhere to run; all Conor could do was drop to his knees and cover his head as the flood crawled over him. Tiny fingernails poked his scalp and neck and picked at his shirt. Conor waved his hand ax in the air, hoping it would frighten them off, but it did little good.

Fingers reached into his pockets and under his shirt. Probably searching for food, Conor realized. He held his satchel tightly to his chest. Inside it was the Granite Ram of Arax. That was a treasure he would lose his life defending, if need be. He dropped his hand ax and used his shepherd's crook instead to ward off any baboons that got too close. At least the monkeys saw him as an obstacle, rather than a target – if they decided to attack, this horde could rip them all to shreds.

Rollan cried out. Conor looked up, his vision nearly obstructed by the mass of baboons. First he saw Briggan, shaking every once in a while like he was drying from a swim, each ferocious quiver sending any baboons that had crawled onto him flying off. Tarik and Lumeo were faring better. Tarik was picking the monkeys off like ticks and throwing them away from him. Lumeo was latched onto his head, swiping his claws at any baboons that came too near.

Rollan, though, must have lost his footing – he was sprawled on his back, covered in the baboons that were tromping over him. He held something aloft, desperate to keep it out of the monkeys' reach – the Coral Octopus of Mulop.

Conor edged toward him, but every place he tried to put his foot seemed to already have a monkey underneath. All he needed was to fall over too. Then the baboons could steal the Granite Ram and the Slate Elephant along with the Coral Octopus.

A cry broke the night sky, and suddenly Conor's view was full of falcon feathers. Essix soared in and plucked a baboon from Rollan, flew a few feet away, and dropped it into the frenzied mass before heading back for another. There were plenty of baboons to replace each one she removed, though, and Rollan was having more and more trouble keeping the talisman away from the swarm. An elderly baboon, with ragged ears and drooping lips, lunged for it.

"Essix!" Conor called. "The talisman! Grab the talisman instead!"

On her next pass, the falcon went straight for Rollan's hand. Her talons clenched the Coral Octopus's rawhide cord, and then she was aloft. She hung a dozen feet up in the air, wings beating furiously. Conor sensed her indecision; surely what she wanted most was to save Rollan – but the Coral Octopus was even more important. The baboons, lustful at the sight of the shiny treasure, made running leaps and tried to catch it, but they came far short each time.

None of the baboons wanted the treasure enough to break off their southerly journey, though. They'd make a few lunges, then move on. The horde began to thin out, and Conor was able to pick his way along the ground to Rollan's side.

The last baboons were the youngest, small juveniles that scampered to catch up to their parents. One tiny baboon ran up Tarik's back, only to be rewarded with a swipe across the face from Lumeo's paw. It squeaked in surprise, then scampered off into the night to catch up to its troop.

"That," Rollan said, panting, "was *insane*." With a cry of agreement, Essix dropped the talisman, then landed on a nearby branch and began preening her baboon-ruffled feathers back into order.

Conor handed the Coral Octopus back to Rollan, then secured the Slate Elephant in his satchel, alongside the Granite Ram. He then checked himself and Briggan for wounds. They had plenty of scratches, and Briggan's eye was half-lidded where it must have been poked, but there were no serious injuries.

"We need to find some shelter," Conor finally said to Tarik.

"Perhaps I can help," came a small voice out of the darkness.

Tarik jerked in surprise and Rollan leaped into the air, Essix right beside him, screeching and beating her wings. Barely having caught his breath, Conor struggled to get his hand ax out and at the ready. "Who's there?"

Conor thought he recognized the voice, but it wasn't until she emerged into the torchlight that he realized who it was for sure. "Irtike?"

The skinny Okaihee girl looked worn and tired, hobbling forward on scratched bare feet. "Yes," she said simply, clasping her hands at her waist.

"Did you follow us all the way from your village?" asked Conor.

She nodded. "The chieftain ordered me to stay. But my mother was . . . If you're going into Conqueror territory, I want to go with you. My heart lives outside of Okaihee now."

Tarik's face was unreadable, but Rollan vigorously shook his head.

"Absolutely not," he said. "You can't come with us. We've been going slowly enough." He looked at Tarik, who seemed to still be considering. "She's not even wearing any shoes, Tarik!"

Irtike spoke evenly and calmly. "I followed you easily enough, didn't I? In fact, I left hours after you did, and picked up your trail with no problem. Yours especially, Rollan. To find you, all I had to do was listen for someone howling in fear under a pile of monkeys. So who here is the liability?"

At first Rollan's face turned red, but then he broke out laughing. "Well played, Irtike."

Irtike continued. "You've been moving at night. I can understand why you would, since you don't want to be detected by the Conquerors. But you've been very fortunate to have survived so far. The Conquerors have been doing more than destroying villages – they've been force-feeding their Bile to animals, making them into powerful monsters that will attack anyone on sight. And I shouldn't have to tell you that some of the most dangerous animals in southern Nilo are nocturnal. Leopards, lions, spiders, and snakes."

"Briggan's sense of smell keeps us safe," Conor said proudly.

"A sense of smell won't keep you from stumbling into quicksand. In Nilo, quicksand can drown a steer in seconds."

"And what, you can sense quicksand in the nighttime?" Rollan asked incredulously.

"Yes, I can," Irtike said simply. "You definitely need me."

"What is *with* the people from Okaihee?" Rollan asked, shaking his head. "So pushy."

"Irtike," Tarik said. "How exactly can you sense quicksand?"

The girl lowered her eyes shyly. "The year before she died, my mother presided over my eleventh nameday. She had me drink the Nectar of Ninani, and I summoned a spirit animal. I am the first since Abeke to do so." She turned to Tarik and bowed her head. "I hoped the Greencloaks might come for me one day."

"I suspect we would have, if we'd known," Tarik said. "But I wonder: You summoned a spirit animal, and yet Pojalo didn't consider you a candidate for the village Rain Dancer. He didn't even mention your animal. What did you summon?"

Irtike reached into a fur-lined leather bag slung across her chest and came out with cupped hands. She moved into the torchlight before she opened them. The companions slowly peered in.

Rollan yelled in disgust. "*Ahh!* What is that?!"

Conor had to force himself to keep his eyes on the creature. It had to be the ugliest living thing he'd ever seen. It was the size of a rat – maybe it even *was* a rat – but it was totally hairless. Its skin was a gooey pink color that transitioned into jaundiced yellow wherever it folded. The eyes were covered by pale membranes that made them look like ticks burrowed under the skin. The monstrous little creature had two long yellow teeth sticking out of its lower jaw. They gnashed as it sniffed the air.

"I guess you roll the dice when you summon a spirit animal, and take what you get," Rollan said. "Sometimes you roll snake eyes. Or, whatever kind of eyes those are."

"Enough!" Irtike said, her brows knitted tight. "He's the reason I've been able to follow you so easily. Not that I'd have had trouble following *you*, He-Who-Shrieks-At-Baboons."

Conor forced himself to look at the creature again. "He helps you follow? But he's . . . blind," he said.

"Exactly," Irtike said proudly. "Naked mole rats usually spend their lives underground. Sensing vibrations is how they know the world, because there's no light down there."

"Sensing vibrations is no better than Briggan's sense of smell," Conor said defensively.

Irtike stroked the mole rat's back. He lifted his wet nose into the air in pleasure, managing to get even uglier in the process. "That's not true," Irtike said. "Did Briggan allow you to *smell* that there's a sheer cliff face fifty yards ahead? I don't think so. My spirit animal is a leader among the mole rats. Like ants or bees, they live as a hive. He can call on other nearby mole rats to aid him. He also grants me the power to move the earth itself."

Rollan went so pale it was visible even in the torchlight. "There's a cliff face fifty yards ahead?"

Irtike smiled with satisfaction. "Who's ugly now?"

"Oh, I'll admit that your little monster is useful," Rollan said. "But I'll never admit that he's anything less than one hundred percent ugly." He glanced at it again, and shuddered. "Gah!"

"Which direction do you suggest we go?" Tarik asked.

"So I may go with you?" Irtike said shrewdly.

Conor found himself nodding before he even considered the question. Tarik paused, then also gave a quick nod. Rollan crossed his arms over his chest.

"Very good," Irtike said. "I'll tell you. I understand why you wanted to go into the jungle. The Conquerors can't patrol it well, and you'd be under cover. But even Essix wouldn't be able to see from above that the jungle floor is full of muddy cliffs and quicksand. It's impassable. You'd die trying to cross it."

"What do you suggest instead?" Conor asked.

"The baboons can go due south," Irtike said, "because they travel in the treetops. Through my mole rat I sensed hoofbeats earlier. They veered left along here, then continued south a mile farther. That seems to be where all the land-bound creatures are heading. There must be some passable route that way."

"And thus, we should follow their path," Tarik said. "Do you agree, boys?"

Conor nodded. Rollan gave an almost imperceptible nod, shifting his dagger at his belt.

"And so it will be," Tarik said softly.

Irtike leaned her ear next to the mole rat, then looked back up. "I can sense a softness in the soil a half mile east of here. Usually that means a fallen tree. We can probably shelter beneath it safely."

"A wise plan," Tarik said. But then he clasped Irtike's shoulder and looked at her seriously. "You've made a courageous choice, to leave the only place you've known and follow us. But you should know that this quest could put you in grave danger. We've lost good friends to this war, Irtike. People much too young have been taken from us, perhaps forever. No one would fault you for changing your mind."

"Thank you," Irtike murmured. "But I'm sure of my choice. The war is everywhere here in Nilo, and I've lost my mother to it as well. I will travel with you and do what little I can to help."

Tarik nodded, his expression solemn. He seemed reluctant to let go of Irtike's shoulder, but eventually he pulled away, giving Lumeo a scratch under the chin with a sad smile.

"Say," Rollan said, finally plucking up the courage to look at the mole rat again. "What name did you come up with for your little monster?"

Irtike shrugged. "Pojalo said he would be the one to choose a name. But he never got around to it. How did you come up with your animals' names?"

"Briggan and Essix were named long before any of us were born," Tarik said. "Lumeo is the brightest thing in my life, so his name was obvious to me, from the root word for *light*." The otter curled tighter around the back of Tarik's neck, nuzzling the underside of his chin. "Most spirit animals like to have some say in their own naming. They are not pets. They're partners."

"I don't know," Irtike said, looking at her mole rat. He bobbed his head in the torchlight. "I'm not that good at coming up with names. And I can't exactly ask him."

"Snake Eyes it is, then," Rollan said. "Hi there, Snake Eyes." The mole rat bobbed his head in Rollan's direction, his blind eyes pointing toward the boy. His blotchy, naked flesh went stiff, wrinkling and folding whenever the mole rat moved.

Rollan gagged. "Wow," he said, heaving in air. "It's worse than a walrus. I never thought I'd say it, but the thing looks *even worse than a walrus*."

"Come on," Tarik said, snuffing out the torch. "Let's move toward the fallen tree Irtike located. I'd like us to be safely hidden away before dawn comes."

Conor tapped his lips. "I think Irtike and . . . Snake Eyes should be with me in the front. The breeze is at our backs, so Briggan and I can only smell what's behind us. We'll know if there are any more animals streaming from the north, but that's about it."

Tarik nodded. "Let it be so."

"There's really no need to worry, everybody," Rollan said. "If we meet any wild beasts on the way, we'll sic Irtike's *mole rat* on them."

They started forward again. Letting his senses merge with Briggan's, Conor felt the night come alive. He smelled nestlings in the treetops and seeds blown from the grasses in the night winds, and earthworms burrowing up toward the starry sky.

All the while, he and his friends moved quietly over the savannah, toward Cabaro.

Toward the lion's lair.

4

DREAM

MEILIN'S DREAM BEGAN WITH JHI. HERE WAS THE WIDE, furry body, and two soft round ears. Arms open, ready to embrace her.

She floated to the panda. Once she was near enough, Meilin reached out and fell deep into Jhi's pillowy warmth. At once tender and strong, the bear's arms reached around her, cradling her like a child, claws tight against Meilin's back.

Words passed from Meilin's mind to Jhi's: *Don't you hate me now, for my betrayal?* She'd never asked that before. Why hadn't she asked Jhi something so important?

The panda stared at Meilin with her wide, expressive eyes, full of compassion. Jhi didn't hate her. She must have been the last being in Erdas that didn't – Meilin included.

She wanted to sink deeper into the comfort of Jhi's soft embrace. *I am weak and powerless,* she wanted to say. *I need you to protect me.* But Meilin was a warrior, and even now couldn't bring herself to say that. She didn't need to, though: Jhi knew what she needed. The panda's arms tightened around her even more, and for a moment Meilin relaxed. But then she saw a new feeling enter Jhi's ordinarily placid eyes: fear.

A foul wind picked up. It pulled on her hair, then ripped Meilin from her spirit animal's grasp. Her fingers desperately raked Jhi's ribs as she was wrested away. Jhi's wide silver eyes stared at her unblinkingly, the last thing Meilin saw in the darkness until they too faded from view.

Meilin slowed and stilled. Shapes formed at the murky edges of her dream and came together to reveal a man in a horned helmet, his thick arms crossed. The Devourer.

Instantly Meilin fell into her fighting stance. A quarterstaff appeared in her hands – the training bo that she hadn't seen since her youth, with grips of white cotton, stained brown in places by blood leaked from calloused knuckles – and immediately she went on the offensive. She began a combo sequence she'd once used to best her father himself in a sparring test. Jab jab roundhouse slash, jab jab roundhouse ankle.

The Devourer had a quarterstaff in his own hands now, and blocked each move with the very ones her father had once used, until Meilin dropped low, ready to uppercut. If this went like before, this was when she'd win.

But now the Devourer didn't do what her father had once done. He crouched low, like her, so that suddenly Meilin found herself staring right into the gaping black eyeholes of his mask.

They froze there, motionless, the Devourer tilting his head left and right, staring into Meilin's soul. She wanted to raise her arms to attack, but was powerless. A glow entered her vision, and she saw something shining green at the Devourer's throat. The light was chilly and beautiful. A totem shaped like a coiling beast faced her, carved from bright stone. The Jade Serpent of Gerathon.

Meilin watched in horror as talisman's face turned to stare at her. As its mouth opened.

Those blank serpentine eyes filled Meilin's vision, and then the beast was Gerathon herself, only smaller, the same size as Meilin. The cobra unhinged her mouth, and giant fangs filled the dreamspace when the serpent lunged. Meilin managed to get her hands around its neck before the fangs reached her, and was sprayed instead by a yellow-green fluid.

Bile.

It was all over her face and throat. She retched at the reek of it, and the Bile burned wherever it had contacted her skin. But she managed to keep her hands around Gerathon, right below her fanged mouth.

Meilin squeezed. Even as she did, she put a thought together: *The Jade Serpent of Gerathon. That's where the Bile comes from.*

Enraged, Gerathon opened her mouth to bite, and Meilin saw only red and bone. But she managed to keep her grasp on the thrashing beast. Sweat dotted Meilin's brow as the scaly cords of muscle under her hands shivered and struggled.

Even as Gerathon thrashed, Jhi appeared behind her, her soft placid eyes staring into Meilin's. Jhi was begging her to stop. *I can't!* Meilin wanted to cry out. *Gerathon is attacking me!*

Jhi's compassion came over her in waves, and Meilin's hands involuntarily relaxed, her grip loosening.

Gerathon struggled to make words. When the sound came out, it was a strangled rasp: *When Nectar bonds a human and animal, neither is in charge. Bile is stronger than Nectar, because it allows one will to dominate. You have always striven for mastery, Meilin. You should allow yourself to dominate Jhi, and the rest of your companions. Your caring lessens you.*

Meilin's hands itched to squeeze again, to kill Gerathon while the serpent was at this small size, and under her hands. She tightened her fingers, when suddenly Jhi attacked – not Gerathon, but Meilin! Her paws batted at Meilin's hands, trying to force her to release. The panda bellowed once, a sad and forceful wail.

The shock of it made Meilin release and fall back . . . and come to consciousness on a cold stone floor.

Meilin was in a turret room. A heavy trapdoor was set in the floor, and a single window cut through the thick stone walls, narrowing to an arrow slit. Jhi was right beside her, her paw on Meilin's arm. Meilin scrambled away, and then saw the panda was relaxed, staring at her in concern. It really had been a dream. Meilin took the panda's paw in her own and exhaled slowly, trying to breathe the nightmare away.

That's when she saw Abeke.

The Niloan girl was laid out on the floor. She'd been savagely beaten. Deep scratches lined her jaw, and her arms were covered in defensive scrapes. Her throat was the worst, though: Wide bruises spread from her windpipe, ending in finger marks that fanned out like violet moth wings.

The fingers were the size of Meilin's.

A wet sob escaped Meilin's lips. She crawled over to Abeke, crouching and nudging her on the shoulders. "Oh, no," Meilin cried. "Please, no. Please wake up, Abeke . . . I'm so sorry!"

Abeke's eyes fluttered open. She saw Jhi and smiled groggily, wincing in pain.

Then Abeke saw Meilin, and her eyes widened in fear. She tried to stagger to her feet, but fell. Abeke pressed her back to the wall, holding her hands up protectively.

"No, Abeke, it's okay!" Meilin said. "It's me, just me. I won't hurt you. I swear."

Abeke slowly lowered her hands. Her body stayed rigid, though, her eyes wary. Meilin watched her friend fight to calm herself. "Meilin," Abeke said, her voice croaking and hoarse. "You were possessed again. You attacked me."

Meilin nodded gravely, wringing her hands. "I dreamed I was fighting Gerathon. I talked to her. I couldn't see you, but I . . . thought it was her I was strangling. Jhi tried to warn me, but I was so confused. I'm sorry, Abeke. I'm so sorry."

"It's not your fault," Abeke said quietly. "I understand that. But I only barely fought you off. I called your name, but you weren't reacting. It was like you couldn't hear me."

"I couldn't," Meilin said. She placed a hand on Jhi and the panda grunted in sympathy, looking at the two girls with her usual placid expression. "It was only because of Jhi that I was able to stop at all. How long was I . . . not myself?"

"I don't know," Abeke said. She dabbed experimentally at her neck wounds. "I woke up to you attacking me."

Meilin put her face in her hands. "That's so terrible."

"I almost summoned Uraza," Abeke said. "But I didn't know what she would do. I was afraid she would attack you."

"You should have," Meilin said, looking at Abeke's wounds. "I can't believe I did that to you. I'd have deserved whatever Uraza did to me."

Studiously avoiding Meilin's gaze, Abeke eased to her feet, then padded gingerly to the window. "It's too bad this faces the outside, not the courtyard. All I can see are a dense mangrove forest and the edge of some buildings leading to docks. Judging from the sandstone walls and the trimmed mangroves, Shane was telling the truth: We're in a wealthy Niloan manor."

Not knowing what to say, Meilin ran her fingers through Jhi's fur. The panda grunted with pleasure.

They'd been in their cell two days, with nothing to eat or drink but one bucket of watery oats Shane had brought. Meilin wished she knew what the Devourer had in mind. Maybe it was simply to keep them out of the way while the Conquerors tracked down the remaining talismans. But from what she was learning about Gerathon, imprisonment wasn't really her style. If all she wanted was to get them out of the way, they wouldn't be in a cell. They'd be dead.

"We know Kovo was the mastermind behind the first great war," Meilin said. "But I think it's Gerathon's talisman that actually creates the Bile. I saw it."

"This could be useful information," Abeke said. "I didn't consider that you might be learning about Gerathon, that your possession might work two ways."

"I didn't either," Meilin said, shrugging. "But Jhi kept showing up in my dream. My connection with her might be what allows me to reverse the direction, to empathize with Gerathon, in some strange way." Meilin didn't sense the serpent in her mind now, which meant the possession probably wasn't permanent – Gerathon must have to intentionally enter her mind, not live there always.

"What we have to do," Meilin continued, "is get the Conquerors to let you near Shane. He's got a weak spot for you. We can use him to get us close to Gar."

"Close to the Devourer? That's what you want?"

"Yes. Close enough to kill him."

Abeke looked at Meilin curiously. "I don't think we stand a chance, Meilin. This place has to be crawling with Conquerors. Our best hope is to escape and find the others."

Meilin stared at her fists. "That's *your* best hope, Abeke, and I plan on making sure it happens. But I can't run away. I'm a danger to you – it's my fault you're even in this mess. All I can hope is to strike quickly and provide enough of a distraction for you to escape."

Abeke opened her mouth to protest, but paused.

She knows I'm right, Meilin thought.

They settled into an uncomfortable silence. For a few minutes Jhi licked the wounds on Abeke's neck, and

Meilin was heartened to hear Abeke sigh in relief. Then, once she'd healed Abeke as much as she could, Jhi sprawled out between the girls like a rug, looking from one to the other and back again.

Sometime later, when the sun was high in the sky, they heard a sound from the trapdoor. It opened an inch, and a familiar voice called out.

Shane.

"I'm coming up. But you should know that there are a half dozen guards with me. So don't try anything."

The girls exchanged a look, and Meilin nodded her assent.

"Okay," Abeke said. "We won't."

"And no spirit animals," Shane said. "If I see them out, I lock the trapdoor and leave."

Meilin nodded again at Abeke. "Uraza is already dormant," Abeke called. "Meilin's taking Jhi into her passive form now."

Meilin held out her arm and nodded to Jhi. The panda stared back at her, her jaw moving back and forth, like she was chewing bamboo. Meilin shook her arm. "Jhi! I'm not kidding around!"

Jhi kept staring. Meilin knew she could force the panda to go dormant, but she had never seen Jhi resist like this. A horrible thought struck her: Maybe Jhi didn't trust her anymore.

"Please, Jhi," Meilin pleaded. "Don't make me do it."

Jhi stayed motionless, but the silver eyes that met Meilin's were full of accusation. The message was clear: Only one of them could *make* the other do anything.

Meilin took a deep breath, summoned all her will, and

compelled Jhi to go dormant. It felt strange and awful, like she was jamming her best friend into a box two sizes too small. There was a burning sensation on Meilin's arm and Jhi was gone, replaced by a tattoo. Meilin imagined that even the tattoo panda was looking at her reproachfully.

Abeke watched Meilin in silence for a moment, her expression somewhere between pity and horror. "Okay," Abeke said finally, averting her eyes. "Our spirit animals are away."

Shane poked his head in. All Meilin could see of him were two eyes and a fringe of blond hair. "Against the wall," he ordered. "Um, please."

The trapdoor opened farther, and Shane hopped off the ladder and into the cell, his tall frame reaching from the floor almost to the ceiling. Abeke and Meilin stared at him. Meilin could sense Abeke's softness, and it worried her. Even if Shane was the kindest of their captors, Abeke needed to be using him, not falling for him.

Shane stood there, arms crossed over his powerful chest, his saber prominent at his hip. "So . . ." he said, trailing off awkwardly. He coughed. "My uncle has summoned you to an audience. I've been asked to bring you to him."

"And if we refuse?" Abeke asked.

Shane cast his eyes to the floor, as if in pain. "Please don't refuse. The moment you refuse to do something Uncle Gar asks, I've been ordered to kill you."

5

THE NARROW PASS

THROUGHOUT HIS CHILDHOOD, CONOR HAD TO GET UP IN the dark to tend to his family's sheep. Over the years his body had learned to spring alive the moment the night bleached even a bit, waking him during the bruised half hour before dawn.

Now he and his friends traveled by night and slept during the day: Dawn was the very moment he was supposed to go to bed. Conor was finding it difficult.

After several sleepless days in the open, they'd finally managed to find shelter in a deserted village. Conor didn't need to imagine why it had been abandoned – they'd already passed squads of Conquerors transporting captured Niloans. They carted village animals too: Some growled and screeched from inside their reinforced cages, enlarged and slathering, corrupted by Bile.

It would have been hard enough for Conor to fall asleep at the very time of the day his body usually woke up. But after all he'd seen in the last days, it was nearly impossible.

Long trails of human beings, starving and suffering. Fields aflame, set on fire by the Conquerors to force the people who had worked them for generations to flee.

Conor lay in a partially charred hut, with a big section of the thatched roof burned away to reveal the gray-black sky. Rollan and Tarik were already snoring, Lumeo snuggled down in the space between them. Irtike lay quietly on her back, eyes closed, Snake Eyes dozing at her collar. Conor didn't know her well enough to be able to tell whether she was really asleep or just hoping for it.

Essix was tracing wheels in the sky, only occasionally coming into view through the gaping roof. The falcon, as ever, was essential for keeping them safe while they rested.

Conor wished for sleep. With one hand in Briggan's fur, he lost himself in the wispy, pinking clouds, a few pinpoints of stars still visible behind them. He relaxed.

Until the birds came.

At first Conor didn't know what he was hearing. The sky filled with a dull buzzing, and then the animals began to rush past, heading south. Conor thought it was a flock of swallows – he'd seen them fly past his village in Eura twice a year, blackening the sky for a few minutes on their way to distant places. But these weren't swallows. They were too small, almost the size of insects.

Then he realized what he was seeing: hummingbirds. Thousands of hummingbirds in glittering blues, greens, and reds, flocking through the sky.

Parrots followed, bright green except for the occasional orange blur, all single-mindedly flying south toward Cabaro's oasis, one nearly on top of the next.

Conor considered waking up the others, but they were sleeping so soundly, and needed their rest. So he watched the unfurling fabric of greens and oranges, listened to its squawking roar.

He must have fallen asleep, because sometime in the middle of the afternoon Conor was awakened by a strange tearing noise, like someone was ripping apart a shirt. Conor shot bolt upright and came face-to-face with Essix. The falcon was sitting in the scrap of bare earth that was still available in the small hut, making a meal of a parrot. Conor turned his face away and closed his eyes. "Essix, come on, can't you do that outside?"

When he looked back, the parrot was eaten, bones and all, and Essix was peering at Conor with quizzical eyes, head tilted. *What's the big problem?*

Conor wondered why Essix was no longer in the sky, but he didn't have the kind of shorthand with the falcon that Rollan did. So he was relieved when Essix woke Rollan up by giving him a swift peck.

"Hey!" Rollan said, sitting up and rubbing his cheek. He looked at Essix's expression, watching as the falcon cast her gaze outside. Rollan's own face went from furious to intrigued. "Wake up Irtike and Tarik," he said. "It seems Essix has found something we should see."

They were mobilized and on the move within minutes. In the daylight, Conor and Irtike took the middle, with Tarik leading and Rollan at the rear, long dagger in hand. There were enough stands of baobab trees dotting the landscape that they could take shelter as they went, hiding in the shade and waiting for Essix's piercing cry to let them know it was safe to make the trek to the next hiding spot.

Essix leading the way, the companions began to ascend, following a rocky dry streambed through yellow nettles until they were on a rise. After hiding themselves in a tuft of tall, dry sawtooth grass, they eyed a narrow pass through the cliffs.

"Oh," Rollan whispered. "That's . . . How awful."

The pass was the only way through the cliffs for miles around, and it showed. There had clearly been many recent bloodbaths. Carcasses lined the sides, the bodies of everything from warthogs to hyenas to monitor lizards. Even humans. The narrow path that remained was rust-colored, the sand and stones soaked in blood.

"How did all those creatures die?" Conor asked.

"I think we're about to find out," Tarik said, pointing to the entrance of the narrow pass.

A herd of wildebeests was approaching, kicking up a cloud of heavy brown dust in the dry savannah. As they neared, a group of mounted Conquerors, clad in their black oiled leather uniforms and sewn-on breastplates, emerged from a hiding spot in the cliff side and began to ride along with them. They expertly navigated the sprinting mass, seamlessly joining the wildebeests.

As the herd neared the pass, it didn't slow at the bottleneck. Wildebeests were crushed against the side of the canyon or lost under stampeding hooves. "That's why all those animals died," whispered Conor. "They've gone mindless. It's terrible."

"I don't think that's all that's killing them," Irtike said, pointing at the far end of the pass.

Ostriches emerged from their own hiding places at the far cliffs, standing in a straight line before the stampeding wildebeests and the Conquerors among them. Once the first animals neared, the ostriches turned so their backs were to them. They peered over their tail feathers and each lifted a leg, as if taking aim. Conor cringed, waiting for the powerful birds to strike out at the witless wildebeests.

"Really?" Rollan asked. "Attack ostriches? Is that a thing?"

"Ostriches are some of the deadliest animals in all of Nilo," Tarik said grimly. "Watch and learn."

The first wildebeest arrived at the ostrich line. The birds didn't attack it, though – they let the animal pass right between them.

When the first Conqueror on horseback arrived, however, the nearest ostrich used one burst from its wings to rise into the air. Its leg lashed out, thick muscles evident even from a distance. The clawed foot struck the Conqueror squarely in his helmet and he went flying, impacting the cliff wall with a thud audible even over the stampede. The helmet was dented all the way in; the Conqueror must have been killed instantly.

His steed, though, was allowed to pass right through. The horse joined the herd of wildebeests, at least those that had survived trampling, and streamed out to the south.

The next Conqueror to reach the ostrich line tried to veer away, but the wildebeest herd was tight around her.

She was drawn forward and met a similar end, kicked in the head by an ostrich. Even Tarik had to look away.

Eventually the Conquerors were all felled, their horses liberated, and the surviving wildebeests were a cloud in the far distance. The ostriches retreated to either side of the canyon.

"Now," Rollan said, "anyone want to tell me what for the love of Mulop just happened?"

"I have a theory," Conor said.

"So do I," Tarik said, nodding approvingly. "Go on, tell yours first."

"Clearly the Conquerors joined that herd intentionally. They thought they could pass by the ostriches if they were intermingled with wild animals. Only it didn't work. The ostriches picked them off."

"Yes," Tarik said excitedly. "Exactly. Only animals are being allowed to pass. But no Conquerors."

"No humans in general," Irtike said, pointing at the bodies at the side of the canyon. "There's tribal clothing down there. Not just Conqueror gear."

"That fits what we know of Cabaro," Tarik said. "He hates humans. Perhaps he wishes for a kingdom in which there are only animals."

"He appears to be getting his wish," Irtike said grimly.

"This cliff goes for miles," Rollan said. "The Granite Ram might get us across, if Essix ferried it between us. Or she could carry us over one by one if we used the Slate Elephant to enlarge her."

"But these ostriches are likely only an advance guard," Tarik said. "Cabaro has made his purpose clear. Humans are not welcome. We will be attacked on sight."

"Not all of us," Conor mused. "Briggan and Lumeo would pass by fine."

"And Snake Eyes," Irtike said defensively, brandishing the mole rat.

"Agh, warn me before you pull that thing out!" said Rollan.

"Right, and Snake Eyes," Conor said, averting his eyes from the hideous creature. "In any case, it's just *people* who have trouble getting through. Like us."

Tarik nodded wearily, peering down at the carnage, his lips a grim line. Conor knew how much the loss of Abeke and Meilin weighed on him, though Tarik never said as much. Conor just wished he had some way of convincing Tarik that he wasn't personally responsible for everything that happened to them.

Conor turned various strategies over in his mind, but none of them held much hope. There was one option left, though clearly no one wanted to say it. Conor hated even the thought of it, but at the same time it seemed the only way forward. He cleared his throat, and the others looked at him. Laying a hand atop Briggan's furry head, Conor scratched between the wolf's ears. Briggan's back leg twitched in pleasure, just like Conor's old sheepdog's would have done. He and Briggan had been parted once before, to save Rollan's life in Pharsit Nang. It had been nearly unbearable. Conor wondered if it was more than his heart could take to do it again. But they had no other choice.

"So that's it, then," Conor said. "We send our spirit animals on. Alone."

6

CABARO

ROLLAN WATCHED CONOR EXPLAIN THE PLAN TO Briggan. The wolf sat at strict attention, his blue eyes never wavering from Conor's. His head would tilt once in a while when he wasn't sure about something, but otherwise the former Great Beast stared deep into Conor's eyes, soaking in every signal he could get off his companion.

Essix, meanwhile, wouldn't be staring dutifully into Rollan's eyes any time soon. No human boy was going to be the boss where a falcon was concerned, and Rollan was just fine with that. She was high in the sky, searching for prey. Irtike carried Snake Eyes close to her, giving the falcon a worried look. He was a perfect Essix-snack size.

Tarik, meanwhile, couldn't stop pacing. Clearly he was no great fan of their plan. It was risky and unusual, and if there was something Rollan had learned about Tarik by now, it was that he liked to do things by the book.

Leaving Essix to her hunting, Rollan went to Tarik's side. "You're not feeling good about this, huh?" he asked.

Tarik crossed his heavy arms. Under the intense Niloan sun, Rollan could see the deep lines around the man's mouth. "Not at all," Tarik sighed. "Cabaro is the most powerful foe we've faced yet. You saw that scraggly lion in Pojalo's hut, and how much trouble it gave us. A full-grown lion might have bested us, and Cabaro is far bigger than a usual lion. Only Suka could rival him for strength, and Cabaro is many times more agile. Briggan might stand a chance in combat if Conor used the Slate Elephant, but even then, wolves must usually work together to bring down larger prey. He'll be outmanned. And Essix . . ."

"She's made for smaller prey too," Rollan said defensively. "It's not her fault. And none of the Four Fallen are as large as the rest of the Great Beasts. But what else can we do? They're the only ones who can approach him without getting kicked in the heads by crazy attack chickens."

"I agree with you," Tarik said wearily. "Which is why I'm allowing this. But all the same, I don't like it."

"Well, we can never know what they're going to find out there. Who knows how Cabaro will react to seeing Briggan and Essix again after all these years?"

Tarik stared out at the desert laid out before them, then unexpectedly laid his hands on Rollan's shoulders. "Rollan. You haven't mentioned Meilin since we left Oceanus."

Rollan's jaw clenched on its own. "Meilin? Why are you bringing her up?"

Tarik ruffled his hair. "You've been distracted the whole time we've been in Nilo. Just a suspicion that she might be on your mind. I know she and Abeke are on mine."

Of course Meilin was on his mind. All the time. But that didn't mean he wanted to *talk* about it.

"We'll find her," Tarik said. "And Abeke."

Rollan doubted it. And even if they did find Meilin, what would they do with her? At any moment Gerathon could take her over and have her beat them to the ground with her hands tied behind her. It all made the prospect getting his friend back pretty bleak. He bit back a caustic reply.

Tarik sighed. "I'm going to tell you something that very few people know. I had a sister once, named Reima. She was three years younger than me, but we were inseparable. Reima was mature, and whip-smart. My parents scrimped and saved just to send her to school. Of the two of us, it seemed she had the brighter future."

Tarik steeled his gaze toward the horizon as he continued. "As you've seen, not all families are happy when a child calls a spirit animal. For most, having a child join the Greencloaks means losing him or her. My parents operated a carpet shop and had counted on me to run it so that they could retire – they were quite old by then. But Lumeo came to me in my Nectar Ceremony, and that changed everything."

At the mention of his name, Lumeo popped his head out of Tarik's bag, peering curiously with his bright eyes. Rollan stroked Lumeo under his chin, and the otter closed his eyes as he basked in the pleasure of it.

"Reima was delighted," Tarik continued. "She loved

Lumeo as much as I did. Secretly I wanted to join the Greencloaks, to use my new link with Lumeo to do good in the world. But I was also ashamed of that dream. Leaving would mean letting my family down. I never shared my hopes with Reima, but she knew. Without my knowledge, she told our parents she wanted to quit her schooling and work in the shop instead. They believed her – and when she took over the family business, I was free to join the Greencloaks."

"She sacrificed her future," Rollan said. "For you."

Tarik nodded and lifted the hem of his cloak into the sunlight. "She gave up much so that I could wear the green. Perhaps too much. Every morning, I silently thank her. Every evening too, before I sleep. She's always on my mind, even though, as I'm sure you've noticed, I don't speak of her. What she means to me, the importance of what she did, is a weight that I keep private. It is mine to bear, and sometimes that makes it seem more pure, more sacred."

Rollan nodded, thoughtful.

"But that's not the only way," Tarik said. "If your burdens become too heavy, you should also know when to share your pain or worries." Tarik placed a hand gently on Rollan's shoulder, smiling softly. "As I've just done with you. You have that option too."

"Okay, old man," Rollan said, ducking from under Tarik's arm. "Keep talking like that and maybe someday I'll become a Greencloak after all."

"Oh, didn't I tell you?" Tarik said. "Those offers expire. Limited time only. Maybe you could try to join next year."

"Right," Rollan said, cuffing him on the shoulder. Then he paused. "You said you *had* a sister. What happened to her?"

Tarik's smile flickered for a moment. "That's a burden I'm not quite ready to part with," he said. "Another time, perhaps."

Rollan nodded.

"Hey, guys!" Conor shouted. "We're ready."

"Essix," Rollan called sharply. "Make room in your head. I'm coming in!" The falcon, busy trying to cave in a particularly promising rodent mound, gave a frustrated cry and then flew to Rollan's shoulder.

"Okay," Rollan said to Tarik, clasping his arm warmly. "Are you sure no Lumeo?"

"There's a broad desert on the other side of the pass," Tarik said. "Lumeo is a water animal. I can't imagine him enjoying that crossing one bit."

"Well, I still think we should send the mole rat," Rollan said dryly. "Every adventuring party needs a mole rat."

"Hey!" Irtike said. "Snake Eyes is too small for this fight. He stays here." From somewhere deep in her bag, Snake Eyes squeaked defiantly.

"Fine, then. Get ready, everyone. I'm going in," Rollan said. He stared deep into Essix's eyes, and felt himself grow lighter. As his sight merged with the gyrfalcon's, there was a curious, tense feeling in his belly. He watched through Essix's precise vision as Tarik took Rollan's own limp body and lay it flat on the ground, placing a bag under his head as a pillow.

Essix took flight, and Rollan's mind was fully in her

light, strong body. His pulse thrummed with joy when they hit the air currents over the canyon.

Rollan's link with the falcon was stronger than ever, but it still only went in one direction. He could see everything the bird saw, and even shared some of her falcon-y instincts, including an innate sense of up- and downdrafts. There was something relaxing to having no control. The only job Rollan had in the world was to experience the thrill of soaring hundreds of feet over the earth.

Essix found a warm updraft and used it to rise higher in the column of air. She was able to control her altitude by easing in and out of the current while she flew. The tight circle of her vision danced around, soon focusing in on Briggan. The wolf loped down the scrubby hill and to the entrance of the narrow passage. He paused, bobbing his head – Rollan could only imagine how strong the carnage below would smell to a wolf – and then Briggan continued forward, not flagging even when the ostriches came out of their hiding places to face him down.

Undeterred, Briggan strode forward. Rollan could sense Essix's shoulder muscles tense as she prepared to dive at the ostriches if they attacked.

The ostriches turned, staring backward, their powerful back legs at the ready. If they struck out, nothing Essix could do would save Briggan – the first foot that connected with the wolf would likely shatter his ribs.

The birds tensed as Briggan loped nearer and nearer, their wings rising as they prepared to take to the air for extra power, their lethal legs cocked and at the ready.

Bird and wolf came closer and closer . . . and then Briggan was in among them.

He went right through. They'd let him pass.

Distantly, from the ears of his own body, Rollan could hear the muffled cheers of Tarik and Conor and Irtike. But Essix wasn't wasting any time celebrating. She left the column of air and glided across the hot desert, keeping Briggan squarely in view below.

Soon after they'd left the cliff passage behind, the desert widened to the horizon. The sky was a brilliant, hot blue. Rollan could feel the heat on Essix's feathers, warming their dark centers and radiating out to the white tips. The nibs retracted into the bird's skin with a prickling sensation, as Essix flattened them so they'd trap less heat.

When Essix peered down at the wolf, Rollan could see that Briggan was having a hard time. The falcon's keen vision caught the dry patches on Briggan's tongue where it lolled heavily from one side of his mouth. He panted as he loped forward, his chest rapidly rising and falling as he shifted his gait into a sort of leaping walk. Rollan could only imagine how hot the sand was under his paws, which were adapted to the dark cool forests of central Eura.

The unending desert was beautiful, but that was a cruel consolation to its true nature. The place was a graveyard. The sand was dotted by the brilliant white skulls and rib cages of the many beasts that hadn't survived their brutal journey south. In the distance Rollan could see what looked like giants' bones, but when Essix focused in, Rollan realized they were strange columns of white minerals. Rollan wouldn't have recognized the material if they hadn't just come from Oceanus – it was coral.

Once, this must have been an ocean. They were the same distance from the pole as Oceanus; maybe Mulop had once swum around here. But now it was desert, and it was the lair of Cabaro.

It was hard to imagine why the Great Lion would want to live out here. It was a barren wasteland, without even scraps of vegetation for shade. Hidden away from the human world, yes, but hardly a suitable stronghold for a Great Beast.

Essix's attention went more and more frequently to Briggan. Rollan could see why the falcon was worried. The wolf was slowing. Not too noticeably, not yet, but if stalwart Briggan was dragging, he must be suffering indeed. Surrounded by the skeletal reminders of the animals that hadn't survived the journey, Rollan wondered if perhaps they should cancel their plan and bring Briggan back.

But then, right in front of Rollan, Briggan doubled in size. The wolf seemed as surprised as he was, skidding in the sand and nearly falling flat on his face. Then Briggan stood, shook his fur free of dust, and started forward again, this time at twice the speed.

Of course, Rollan thought, *Conor just realized he should put on the Slate Elephant. Why didn't we come up with that before?* Maybe Tarik had been right that Rollan was distracted by thoughts of Meilin these days.

In his new giant form, Briggan actually seemed to enjoy the journey. He quickened his strides, leaping between dunes. Clearly no longer as worried, Essix's gaze flicked over the many skeletons they passed, maybe looking for stray bits of sun-dried meat.

As Essix soared over the unchanging desert, riding waves of dry heat, Rollan lost track of time. He only snapped out of his dreamy state when a speck of green appeared on the southern horizon. It grew larger and larger, until Essix's keen vision was able to make out dense clumps of bright green palms, surrounded by thickets of vines and rubbery bushes, birds and monkeys scampering between the fronds. Many tracks circled the ring of precious greenery.

An oasis.

It was large, hundreds of yards across. There must have been some sort of spring in the middle to provide so much lushness in the middle of the desert. A semicircle of sandstone cliffs curled around the back of the oasis, rising high above it. The beautiful ring of green was probably easy to defend, since intruders could approach from only one direction.

Essix descended, coming in to glide onto Briggan's back. The falcon cried out, and the wolf shifted his ears affirmatively. It seemed Briggan already knew what Essix was telling him. He had probably scented the oasis and figured out precisely what they were heading for.

This lush stand of greenery below the cliffs, so highly defensible, was where Cabaro had secreted himself away.

At first Rollan couldn't understand why Essix didn't rise back into the air, but as the trees rose into view, he realized how dense the foliage was. If the falcon had gone back to flying, she would have lost sight of Briggan the moment he stepped into the oasis.

It was a frustrating way to travel. Essix bobbed with each step Briggan took, sending the falcon's already jerky vision bouncing. Rollan started feeling sick to his stomach.

As they neared the oasis, Rollan recognized an elderly baboon with raggedy ears hanging in the trees, one of the same baboons that had swarmed them outside Okaihee. Once Briggan was near, the chattering creatures in the trees fell silent, and Rollan became intensely aware of their stares. Other heads emerged from between the thickets – wild dogs. The monkeys and birds fled in unison, deeper into the oasis. The dogs remained, watching the wolf nervously. Still enlarged by the Slate Elephant, Briggan was many times their size, and it seemed to have them spooked.

Briggan arrived at the oasis line, and the landscape went from empty to overfull. Water-greedy plants clogged the ground so thickly that there was no clear path for him to follow. Rollan debated returning to his own body to tell the others that Briggan was too big to enter, but decided against it. Better to give Briggan a chance to figure out a way to enter without shrinking him back to his normal size. He'd need every advantage he could get to stand a chance against Cabaro.

Sure enough, Briggan figured out a way in. The giant wolf reared on his back legs and came down on the nearest palm. Essix shrieked and took to the air as, with a great crash, the tree plummeted into the foliage, flattening the surrounding palms. Briggan picked his way along the fallen trunk and then downed another palm, Essix flapping above him the whole time. After a noise like that, every animal in the oasis had to know exactly where they were. Though he'd given up the element of surprise, Briggan had found an effective way of traveling through the oasis.

Essix nipped Briggan's ear in warning. The wolf turned, and Rollan could see that the dogs at the oasis's edge had assembled and were tailing him, crying nervously and sniffing the ground. They were small and mangy, with numerous scabby hairless spots, but there were plenty of them – at least a dozen, maybe as many as twenty. Rollan knew why Essix was concerned, but couldn't see what was to be done about the persistent dogs. At least they weren't attacking – yet.

As Briggan continued his passage, the oasis was eerily still. The advantage of Essix's vision was gone in the thick greenery – all Rollan could see were clustered leaves and the blurred legs of scurrying creatures. Beneath it all he heard Briggan's exhausted panting and the soft howls of the tailing dogs.

Finally Briggan crashed a tree that didn't lead to more greenery. The wolf stepped cautiously into a clearing.

After all that sand and heat, the oasis's center was impossibly beautiful. Water burbled and spilled from the ground in the middle of the clearing, forming a radiant pool. Around it grew bright green mosses and ferns, overhung by desert willows. At the lagoon's edge were peacocks, tail feathers in such striking reds and greens that they seemed bejeweled.

The plump peacocks were of no interest to Essix, though. After the long trip through the desert, Rollan could sense the sole desire burning in her: to drink from the pool. He could only imagine how much furry and panting Briggan wanted to lap up some of that lagoon water too.

They would have gone right for it, if only they'd been alone.

When Essix and Briggan stepped into the clearing, sleek yellow forms picked their way out of the greenery at the far side. Powerful and sinewy, they stalked forward, eyes trained on the wolf, long front teeth displayed in warning. Lionesses, four of them. They came to a stop, a loose clump of fierce cats between Briggan and the lagoon.

Rollan could sense Briggan's indecision. There was no need to attack the lionesses when they weren't attacking him – but the cats were blocking access to the water. Rollan remembered Lenori mentioning something else about lions. Where there was a group of lionesses, there was usually a male.

The surface of the lagoon water began to tremble and shake. Moving sinuously, Cabaro emerged from the foliage at the far side.

He was lean, and *long* – almost half again as long as Briggan, even with the Slate Elephant. Each step Cabaro took around the edge of the lagoon brought him a shocking distance. If this lion went at full speed, there was no land creature on Erdas that could escape him. No wonder he'd been able to keep his Golden Lion talisman safe for so long.

The giant lion sauntered into the midst of his lionesses, then lowered himself calmly onto the sand, tail thumping the earth. He yawned, exposing long teeth – longer even than those of Suka. He might not have the sheer muscle of the giant polar bear, but all it would take was one well-placed chomp from that mouth to be the end of Briggan. And the lion moved so liquidly, with such ease, that it seemed all he'd have to do was decide to bite and then his jaws would be wrapped around Briggan's throat.

For a long moment, Cabaro stared into Briggan's eyes. Rollan could detect a keen intelligence there, a cunning mind churning through possibilities. Then, with a throaty, velvety voice, the Great Beast spoke. "Briggan. Essix. You've come for my talisman."

Casually, Cabaro tossed his mane. When his collar of fur lifted, beneath it Rollan could see a spectacular treasure. The lion was wearing a length of gold rope, gleaming in the light. In the place of pride was a hefty gold figurine, fashioned after a yawning cat.

The Golden Lion of Cabaro.

Languidly, luxuriously, Cabaro tilted his head and licked the talisman again and again, like it was an unruly patch of hair. Then he rested back on his haunches, tossing his mane proudly. It came to rest over the talisman, shielding it from view.

"Of course, you can't reply," Cabaro said. "You are nothing like your former selves. I remember how proud you were, Essix. How regal, how quick-witted. Second only to Halawir the Eagle in the speed of your tongue. You might have convinced me to join your battle against the others, if Halawir hadn't talked me out of it long before you called your Grand Council."

Cabaro's tawny eyes moved from Essix to the wolf beneath her. "And, Briggan – none of the Great Beasts would have claimed you were the smartest among us, but you were loyal to the end, the only one all of us trusted. Few could best you in combat, and certainly not if your Great Pack was behind you. But now you've returned, smaller and silent." The lion's eyes flashed shrewdly. "Yes, I'm aware your size is borrowed. From Dinesh, no doubt. Your new state is sad to see. You are puppets to humankind. Like so many animals. You might as well be pets or milking cows."

Briggan and Essix held still. Suddenly it felt like there was a glass wall within Essix's mind. It was harder for Rollan to know what the falcon was feeling on the other side.

"You are servants of the Greencloaks now, no? *You*, who need bow to no human. They speak of partnerships, of a union of souls. But what are you, really? How many decisions do the Greencloaks turn to their spirit animals to make? They call you up when they want you to risk your necks in combat. They banish you when you are no longer convenient, like a parlor trick. Do you remember the argument we had during the Grand Council? About whether the humans deserved their fate? They have only become bolder. Even more entitled. *You* are the ones with the wisdom hard won through eons of life. And yet you're at the beck and call of humans, who have only the paltry stupidity of decades."

Briggan growled, and Rollan realized he had no idea why. He desperately wondered what was going through the wolf's mind. Did he agree with Cabaro?

"Look throughout Erdas," the giant lion continued, holding up a paw and flicking his long claws in and out. "Cows are kept for milk, subverted to human needs. Pigs are chained, faithfully waiting for scraps until they are killed for a meal. Birds are crammed in cages because humans think they are beautiful. This is not a friendship, nor even the wild freedom of predator and prey – it is a system imposed by human civilization. And you are the firewood that system burns to run. That is why I have secured this oasis. That is why my animal guards kill any human who dares approach."

Cabaro lost his fake calm. The giant lion stood and paced, crossing the clearing and back in a few long strides, keeping Briggan and Essix in his sights the whole time. "This is one region where humans will never come. One place where they cannot chain us, fool us, mock us, dominate us. Once enough allies have arrived, we will expand, and take back the world. I invite you to stay, Essix and Briggan. Join me, and regain control of your destinies."

Oh, no, Rollan thought, swayed by Cabaro's words despite himself. *This could be trouble.* He'd never tried it before, but he tried to funnel thoughts to the falcon. *You are my best friend. We share a soul. I am not using you. And getting the talismans is the only way to stop Kovo and Gerathon and the Devourer. The ones who killed you so long ago. Hiding away here isn't the answer.*

Cabaro came to a stop in front of Briggan and Essix. He was almost in striking distance.

Please, Rollan implored Essix, *we need the talisman. For all of Erdas.*

Cabaro came nearer still, and soon his nose was next to Briggan's. His lips peeled back from his gums, into a wide and toothy grin. "We ended on bad terms, but you always preferred my company to Uraza's, didn't you? Do you remember, Briggan, when we used to hunt in an animal paradise, before humans came and ruined everything? But you've finally come around, haven't you?"

Briggan let out a low growl.

Essix spread her wings and arrowed into the sky. The sudden change in view set Rollan reeling, his stomach in tight knots.

For a moment, the future of Erdas was literally up in the air.

To Rollan's relief, the falcon went directly for the Golden Lion. Within seconds, she had her talons around the back of Cabaro's mane and lifted. If she'd been the one to benefit from the Slate Elephant, she might have been able to yank out the lion's fur and peel away with the talisman. But the heavy gold pendant was too tangled. The falcon faltered.

That was all the delay Cabaro needed. With a roar of rage, the lion turned and pivoted, doing a full rotation in the air and landing a dozen feet away, the talisman still secure. Rollan and Essix waited for the Great Beast to strike.

But, surprisingly, he held still.

Instead, the attack came from the lionesses.

During the commotion, they'd quietly flanked Briggan and Essix, stealing in from both sides. The first to reach Briggan leaped, her fangs sinking deep into his shoulder. Briggan yelped and twisted, but the lioness held on. Then another latched on, her claws raking deep into Briggan's hindquarters, and his howls became anguished.

Essix was a spear of fury, soaring into the air and diving for the first of the lionesses. The fierce cat released Briggan as she was struck in the flank, rolling along the sandy ground and lying still. By then Briggan had managed to twist enough to get another between his jaws. He plucked her from him and hurled her to one side. She too rolled and lay still.

A third lioness took advantage of Briggan's vulnerability to latch onto his throat. Feathers flying, Essix hovered in the air beside her, lashing furiously with her talons. Cuts and gashes accumulated on the lioness's body, but she held on, ears flat and eyes scrunched tight.

Meanwhile, Rollan saw that the wild dogs were accumulating at Briggan's rear, growling and whining. Then the first wild dog clamped onto Briggan's tail. Another sank its teeth into the wolf's foot, heedless of being trampled. A third bit into Briggan's hamstring.

Yelping in confusion, Briggan started sinking. The wild dogs went after his flank – six, then seven, then eight of them latched on, in addition to the exhausted lioness at the wolf's front. Flailing under the combined weight, Briggan began to teeter and pitch. If the dogs pulled him off his feet, he'd be done for. Essix abandoned the lioness and started going after the dogs, picking them off one by one. But each attacker that Essix taloned away was replaced by two more as the pack attacked in full force.

Cabaro, meanwhile, had retreated to the other side of the lagoon. The whole time, he watched and waited, following the action with apparent calm.

His heart in his throat, Rollan could only hope that Briggan and Essix somehow managed to turn the tide before the wolf succumbed.

Then, suddenly, he felt his world shake. In one wrenching and nauseating moment, he lost all his perspective, and the horizon fell away.

Abruptly Rollan was in his own body again. All he could see was Tarik right in front of him, leaning over with a concerned expression.

"What are you doing?!" Rollan shouted. "Briggan and Essix–!"

Tarik clamped a strong hand over Rollan's mouth, his eyes flashing with urgency. "Hush! They'll hear you."

Rollan tried to speak, but the words were unintelligible under Tarik's hand. He bit into Tarik's palm.

Tarik winced, but kept his hand clamped firmly over Rollan's mouth. Then he wrenched the boy to his feet and dragged him to where Conor and Irtike were crouched in the underbrush, staring intently at the narrow canyon pass leading to the oasis.

It was crawling with Conquerors. An army of them.

7

ASSEMBLY

THE LADDER DOWN FROM THEIR CELL WAS RICKETY AND unstable, and in her half-starved state it took Abeke a few seconds to descend it. By the time Meilin was beside her and the trapdoor was closed, Abeke had done a count of the assembled Conquerors: twelve, and five spirit animals. Nearest to her was a mean-looking creature – an animal like a huge orange rabbit, with very strong-looking legs. Perhaps it was from Stetriol, which Abeke figured was bound to have its own sorts of animals, and so its own sorts of spirit animals.

Shane had a burlap sack in each hand. "I'm sorry, but you'll have to wear these to the hall."

Abeke shot a questioning look to Meilin, who nodded slightly. Shane placed the sacks over their heads, and the world went dim. Abeke clasped Meilin's hand, and took comfort in how strongly Meilin held hers in return. Her hands were cool and firm, the callouses from quarterstaff training rough against Abeke's wrist.

As she pressed near, Meilin whispered, "With a sack over my head, at least Gerathon can't see through my eyes."

Abeke squeezed Meilin's palm. "I'm sure Rollan would find a joke somewhere about all this."

"I can only imagine," Meilin said.

Shane took Abeke's other hand. While Meilin's was cool, Shane's was warm and throbbing with life. He tugged Abeke forward almost tenderly, and Meilin followed last, pressed tightly against her friend. Abeke heard the Conquerors fall into line beside them. No one seemed permitted to talk, so all she heard were reverberating footfalls in open stone corridors. Hot Niloan sunshine warmed her arms.

Their footsteps stopped echoing, the stone replaced with grass and sand. Abeke realized they'd passed into a courtyard of some sort. There were rippled murmurs, then all went silent. "Just a few more steps," Shane said as he led Abeke and Meilin across an expanse of open ground. From the sounds around them, Abeke assumed they were in the manor's courtyard.

Abeke felt the warmth of Shane's chest as he leaned over her, and then the sack was off her head. She was right: She and Meilin were at the center of a courtyard that could only have belonged to a member of the Niloan upper crust. Living in Okaihee, Abeke had never seen so grand a home, but she'd heard of the merchant lords whose coastal villas were said to include arenas for sport and theater. Now, though, the baked-earth risers were full of men and women in Conqueror uniforms.

The assembled forces surrounded the two girls, but none made a move toward them. Their eyes were fixed on the front.

A round dais had been set up, on which stood the Conqueror leaders. At one edge was Drina, as beautiful as her brother, Shane, was handsome, but with only glimmers of his reluctant kindness. Her spider spirit animal was perched on her shoulder, motionless. At the other edge of the dais was Yumaris, the old prophetess whose earthworm spirit animal allowed her to scry locations far away. Shane stood behind her, almost hidden from view, looking somewhat sheepish, his arms crossed at his waist.

It was the beast at the center, though, that made Abeke's heart pull down tight in her chest. Gerathon was two tons of snake, black coils rasping as her muscular body curled and twisted in ever-tightening spirals. The giant cobra stared right at them, her face fixed in a leer. A large forked tongue, as wide as the trunk of a man, flicked in and out as she smelled the air. Gerathon opened her mouth, revealing flesh pink and glistening as she extended and retracted her fangs. Even without injecting poison, a strike from those daggers would be enough to kill. The display was meant to intimidate, and it worked.

Abeke panicked. Her whole body seized, and before she could regain self-control she'd summoned Uraza. The leopard sprang to Abeke's feet and immediately started growling, pacing tight circles around her partner. Abeke hadn't felt the pain of summoning her spirit animal for a few days, and the shock of it returned her to her senses. But still–what a horror before them.

The serpent coiled around a massive man, clad in red mail with a horned helmet masking his face; all Abeke could see were two glinting eyes. She'd seen Gar in his full armor only from afar, at the Battle at Dinesh's Temple and the beach when she'd arrived. He would have been looming and impressive in any other context, a formidable opponent for any fighter. But with the serpent mantling him and eyes glinting with wicked intelligence . . . all Abeke could think was that they were doomed.

"Silence!" Gar shouted.

As the crowd's murmurs quieted, Abeke managed to focus her mind. Though Gar was an impressive man, Abeke started to realize how small he looked compared to Gerathon. The Devourer appeared to be in charge, but Abeke suspected how far that went. In Oceanus, Mulop had revealed the truth about the last Devourer, King Feliandor. He was only a puppet to the schemes of Kovo and Gerathon. Maybe the same thing was happening again. If so, she resolved to find a way to use it to her advantage.

Meilin whispered into Abeke's ear, her words coming in a rush, as if she knew this might be their last chance to talk. "Zerif and Aidana aren't here anymore. They might have gone to find Cabaro's talisman. We need to find out where they are."

Meilin sounded like Meilin again! Abeke's heart soared with the sudden hope of it. Meilin had to be intimidated as well, but she was still planning their best moves for the future. Abeke was relieved too, to see Meilin had summoned Jhi. The panda stood on all fours, like Uraza, giving

Gerathon a look of layered anger. Of course the two had a long history, had once been allies – or at least brethren – until Gerathon sent the last Devourer on a mad rampage, and Jhi and Uraza had perished in the conflict.

Gar spoke, and Abeke's mind went back months before, to the day she'd first met him, before she'd joined the Greencloaks. Here was the same light but commanding voice, a grave and compelling sound. "Greencloak children. It is only right that you have brought forth Jhi and Uraza," he said. "They too should see the history occurring around them. They helped shape the world once before, and now they can watch it happen again."

The general removed his helmet, and Abeke saw familiar features under brown-and-silver hair, the circlet across his forehead in the shape of a snake consuming its own tail. Then, she hadn't known what terrible destruction Gar would wreck on the world. Seeing the Devourer now made her body go rigid with fear and anger.

Abeke sensed Meilin go still beside her. This was the first time she was seeing the man who had killed her father.

The Devourer wasn't more than a dozen yards off – even though Abeke had no doubt she would be dead soon after, she could easily have made a shot from this distance. She longed for her bow and arrow.

Drina spoke, and for some reason the moment she started speaking Shane's face went pale. "Uncle Gar, you should have Gerathon *force* them to put away their animals. I've fought Greencloaks, and I know what trickery they're capable of."

Gar chuckled grimly and slapped his fist. "You may

have been defeated by a Greencloak, dear Drina. News of your embarrassment has not escaped me. But that does not mean that any of them could manage to hurt *me*."

Shane shot a concerned look at his sister, imploring her to stay quiet. Abeke studied their interaction, confused and fascinated. She thought Drina was right, actually – it was a mistake to allow them Uraza and Jhi. But all the same, Abeke knew that if she'd interrupted her father at a tribal council, she'd have heard no end of it. Gar had a similar sort of severity to him, and Drina had clearly spoken out of turn.

"You are correct, General," said Gerathon, her voice low and raspy. "It gives me pleasure to see how weak and pitiful Uraza and Jhi look in their new, tiny forms. If only Essix and Briggan could be on display here as well."

"Maybe you'd like Jhi and me to come closer," Meilin said defiantly. "So you can see us better." Her legs locked into a fighting stance.

"Oh, if you wish to be eaten, I can make that happen," Gerathon rasped. "Do not fear."

"If you don't plan to fight us or kill us, there is no other point to this meeting!" Meilin shouted, fury in her eyes. "You will learn nothing from us."

Gerathon disengaged from Gar and writhed, her coils thrashing in smaller and smaller rings. The Great Serpent's dark eyes flashed yellow, and Meilin went slack. Her own pupils dilated. "Rollan," the girl said numbly. "Let me protect you, Rollan."

Abeke's heart dropped in horror at the sight of her friend possessed. Without meaning to, she lifted a hand protectively to her throat.

Meilin's eyes regained their usual luster. She looked like she was waking from a dream, groggy and confused. Then a look of dismay came over her face. "What just happened?" she whispered to Abeke.

"Nothing," Abeke said resolutely.

"Oh, we will learn plenty from you!" Drina called out. "Your Great Beasts are nothing compared to ours."

"Sister, be quiet," Shane said pleadingly.

Meilin hung her head. Abeke suspected what her friend was thinking, and it made her sick: Part of Meilin wished the Conquerors *would* kill her.

"Many months ago, I told you the plight of Stetriol," Gar said, cutting through the laughs and mutterings of the assembled Conquerors. "That the Greencloaks have ignored our continent and left its people to suffer in isolation. And I wasn't lying to you. But we are through *asking* for assistance. A war is underway. Once, Zhong might have given us the most trouble, but we have been victorious there. The royal palace lies in cinders. Amaya and Nilo are falling, and Eura will be ours soon after. It is inevitable which way this war will go, and once it does, Kovo the Ape will be released. Then, with the united talismans, the new age of order for Erdas can begin."

At the mention of Kovo, Meilin perked up.

"History will have only one right side," Gar finished. "You can join us, or you can die!" The Devourer raised his hand triumphantly, and the assembled Conquerors roared.

"Never!" Meilin screamed, tears of frustration and anger in her eyes. "The only fate for the man who killed my father will be death at my hand!"

Abeke held silent, wishing that Meilin could hold back her rage. They would never join the Conquerors, but it might be wise to play along, if it meant staying alive.

Gar chuckled grimly. "I might have expected as much. You probably think of this little show of yours as an act of courage. But I see only foolishness. The tides have turned, and yet you insist on swimming against them. You know what happens to people who swim against tides for too long, don't you? They drown."

He made a great show of laying his hand on the grip of his greatsword. "I will give you one day to change your mind. After that time –"

"*I* will do as I will," Gerathon finished. She opened her wide jaws and extended her hollow fangs from the pink flesh of her mouth. A muscle in her throat flexed, and a drop of poison emerged from each, shining green-yellow in the sunlight.

At the sight of Gerathon's fangs, Abeke experienced a fear stronger than any she'd felt before. It was fear without exit, fear without hope. A pall descended on the courtyard. Even in her panic, Abeke noted it to herself: *The Conquerors are scared of Gerathon, too.*

Slowly, Gerathon retracted her fangs and closed her mouth. A drop of venom was still hanging from her lower jaw; her long forked tongue emerged and flicked it away.

It landed right on Drina's foot.

The girl shook her boot frantically, trying to get the noxious fluid off. Once she had, her lips curled back in disgust. "So foul," she muttered.

At the sound of her words, the assembled Conquerors

went silent. Drina seemed to realize her breach, and put a hand over her mouth.

"Drina," Gar said, breaking the bleak spell holding the audience still. "Step forward."

"What?" Drina said, her voice quavering. She shot a worried look to her brother. He clenched his jaw, eyes wide. He was powerless to help her.

"Step forward," Gerathon hissed, circling her huge body around Drina's ankles, the scales cutting her flesh as Drina struggled to keep her feet. "Do as your lord requests."

Drina staggered toward Gar. The spider on her shoulder skittered around her neck to the other side and back again, agitated. "I'm sorry, General Gar, if I have offended –"

"Now," he intoned. "Come to me."

Abeke watched in dread and confusion as Drina, head hung low, stepped toward Gar. "Hold out your hand," he ordered.

Drina did as she was told, palm up. Her fingers trembled.

"You were tasked with recovering the talismans the Greencloaks have accumulated in Greenhaven. You have failed."

Drina stood motionless and wordless, terror on her face. "Uncle, please!" she cried out. "Their defenses were too strong."

Gerathon's eyes went yellow again, and the spider on Drina's shoulder – her spirit animal – reared back, raising its front legs. Enthralled by the Great Beast, it rocked from side to side, as if it were in an invisible current. Then, it skittered down Drina's body, walking out over her shaking, outstretched arm, until it was at the pale exposed wrist. It paused again, forelegs in the air. In striking position.

"There is only one punishment for failure, niece," Gar said, his voice soft with resignation. "Even for you."

The spider peered at Gerathon with its many eyes, rocking back and forth in its mind-controlled trance.

Almost imperceptibly, the grinning cobra nodded.

When the spider lifted its fangs, Drina's eyes narrowed. Abeke could sense her trying to control her spirit animal.

But the giant arachnid was under Gerathon's control now. Drina must have drunk the Bile, just like all the other Conquerors. Drina gave up on controlling the animal, and instead flailed her arm, trying to get the spider off. It clung on tight, all its legs circling her wrist.

With surprising speed, Yumaris stepped forward. She grabbed the girl's hand and wrenched it cruelly, forcing the arm still. "Now!" Yumaris hissed. "Finish her now!"

"Please, Gerathon–" Shane began to say.

But his words were lost as, silently and cleanly, the spider sank its fangs into Drina's wrist.

Drina bled like she'd been stabbed; the spider's fangs were that large. She gasped at the pain, and her knees buckled. Almost immediately, her eyes fluttered and rolled back. Then she collapsed, quivering, on the ground. Within seconds, she was still.

The assembled Conquerors were queasily silent for a moment.

Then Yumaris raised a cheer, her old voice quavering but loud. "All hail the Reptile King!"

The crowd yelled out, stomping their feet. "All hail the Reptile King!"

Abeke could see fear on many of the Conquerors' faces. None of them wanted to be the next victim of Gerathon's rage. It was then that she realized the truth: This awful display had been as much for the assembled troops as it had been for her and Meilin. Every one of the Conquerors, from their soldiers to their leaders, were prisoners in this war.

They were all Gerathon's puppets.

The only one not joining in the cheering was Shane. He remained silent, his face slack. He took a step toward his sister's slumped corpse, when Gerathon snapped her head toward him, hissing warningly.

"Do not make us suspect that brother is like sister, Shane," she said, barely audible over the crowd's roar. "This is the time for you to prove your loyalty."

"Yes," Shane said, so quietly Abeke could only barely hear him. "You are right."

Shane's head rose, and Abeke was shocked to see him look right past Gerathon – at *her*. Within the tumult of the cheering Conquerors, the creaks of their armor, and the clanging of their weapons, Abeke saw Shane's lips move. It took her a moment to understand what he was saying.

"Six, five, four . . ." He was counting down!

Nothing got past wise old Yumaris, though. Her eyes widened when she saw Shane's lips. "Beware!" she cried, shaking her gnarled staff at him.

The boy sprang into motion, lunging toward Gar. With surprising agility Yumaris stepped into his way, and the two tumbled, rolling into the Reptile King. Gar barely budged at the impact, but the elderly Conqueror didn't get up. Shane was soon on his feet before a stunned Gar, unsheathing his saber and taking a fighting stance. Shane didn't attack his uncle, though: Instead, he sprinted toward Abeke and Meilin.

Uraza darted in front, as if to fight him, but Abeke cried out for her to fall back. The leopard faltered, confused, frozen with one paw in the air, peering at Abeke with her violet eyes. Shane surged past her, tossing his saber to Meilin. She caught it handily.

"They killed my sister," Shane said, his features contorted in rage. "They made her–"

"We saw!" Abeke cried as she crouched, fists out. There was no time to think. The Conquerors were recovering from their surprise and surging forward. If Abeke and Meilin had any hope of escape, they had to act *now*. "Where do we go?"

Shane pointed to one spot in the courtyard. It was swarming with Conquerors, but Abeke would have to trust his judgment that they could somehow escape that way. They dashed across the sandstone flagstones, Jhi taking up a defensive position on one side, Uraza on the other. Meilin whipped the saber through the air while she ran, testing its weight. She was preparing for battle.

Gerathon opened her mouth wide, fangs as long as lances. With muscular side-to-side motions, she arrowed across the courtyard to cut them off. The serpent was horrifyingly fast – she'd be on them in a moment. "Shane . . . !" Abeke warned.

"I know!" he barked.

As soon as they reached the Conquerors at the edge, Abeke realized why Shane had chosen this spot. There were five enemies at one portal, but two lowered their weapons in confusion when they approached – they must have been Shane's friends.

The other three were not.

They fell into defensive positions, crouched with swords raised.

Uraza was on them first. She'd built up a fierce sprint across the courtyard, and hit the nearest Conqueror like a spear, striking his chest and pinning him to the ground. Immediately, she wheeled to face the next. Meilin already had her, though, dropping to her hands for a kick to the Conqueror's knee. She then grabbed the Conqueror's own sword and came up sharp with the hilt, knocking the woman out cold. That left only one blocking their escape route. Again Abeke longed for her bow. But she didn't have it. Without martial arts training like Meilin's, she struggled to figure out how to best contribute to the fight. When the last Conqueror brought her sword blade slicing toward her, Abeke was rooted to the ground.

Shane had it under control. Using his shoulder as a battering ram, he came in sideways, slamming the Conqueror in the gut and rolling to the ground with her. Within a moment the Conqueror was unconscious on the ground and Shane was back on his feet, motioning them forward.

Aware of Gerathon's giant black shape bearing down, Abeke stuck close to Shane's side. Meilin, though, had whirled to face the crowd descending on them, Shane's saber brandished in one hand and the Conqueror's sword in the othcr.

"Meilin, what are you doing?" Abeke cried. But then she saw where Meilin's attention was focused: Gar. The general of the Conquerors, the man who had killed Meilin's father, was marching toward them. Her face furious, Meilin crouched in a fighting stance, her blades held out parallel to the ground.

Jhi stood on her two feet between Meilin and Abeke, looking between the pair of them. Gerathon was nearly in striking distance, and the panda slowly turned to face her. It would be hopeless to try to fight the giant serpent and the Devourer – Meilin had to realize she was putting not only herself, but the rest of them in danger.

"Now isn't the time!" Shane shouted. "If you want to escape, you have to come with me!"

"For Jhi's sake, Meilin!" Abeke cried.

Meilin turned, saw Jhi right in Gerathon's path, and lowered her weapons. Jhi joined her as she ran toward Abeke and Shane, bringing her blades up just in time to parry a Conqueror's mace. She grunted under the impact and fell to the stone floor, then rolled and was back on her feet in an instant.

Shane led the charge through the archway. It gave out into a ditch skirting the exterior wall of the manor house. Uraza followed after, the others racing behind.

"The boat that took you from Okaihee," Shane panted as they ran. "It's my family's ship. It's moored in the harbor, on the far side of this town. If we're the first to get there . . ."

"Got it," Abeke said, breaking into a full sprint.

They passed along the manor's wall, past what looked like the Conquerors' armory, until a large Niloan port town came into view, an assortment of blocky baked-mud buildings leading down to docks. The Conquerors must have all been assembled at the manor courtyard, and they'd managed to break ahead of them – the way forward appeared to be free of enemies. Shane knew just the turns to take through the winding streets, and the tumult behind them began to sound farther and farther away. They raced past shuttered shops, empty dining tents, and unattended training rooms.

Abeke heard seagulls, and realized they must be nearing the dock. Shane began to slow, and led them through an unmarked door into a dank building. He shut the door behind him, then began sifting through stacks of damp, sea-rotted crates piled against a wall. "Before the Conquerors took over this town, this building used to be the customs house," he explained. "I wasn't expecting a voyage, so there won't be any fresh food for our trip. But there's enough to eat and drink in these old shipments, if you don't mind hardtack and *lots* of fermented Niloan cherry. Grab a box, each of you, and we'll head straight for the ship."

While Uraza paced, Abeke took the largest crate she could handle. She followed Shane through the cavernous, musty hall, and only realized Meilin wasn't with her when she reached the far door. She turned and saw Meilin with Jhi, sitting motionless by the crates, head bowed and hands clasped. "What is it?" Abeke said impatiently. "We have to leave *now*, Meilin."

Meilin looked at her, tears in her eyes. "I'm not coming."

"You have to be kidding me," Shane said. "They'll kill you for trying to escape, you know that, right?"

"Gerathon can use me any time she wants. She can make me kill myself, like she forced Drina's spider to kill her. Or she could make me kill Abeke. I can't come with you. It's not safe."

"I don't care!" Abeke said. "I'm not leaving you."

"Think reasonably," Meilin said. "This is for the best. You have no chance if I'm with you. Gerathon will use me to find out where you are. Or worse. Admit it."

Jhi took a step toward Abeke and Shane, looked forlornly at Meilin, then stepped forward again. It was clear she was torn on the matter.

"She has a point, Abeke," Shane said quietly. "Meilin is compromised. You and I never drank the Bile. Our bonds came naturally."

"Meilin, you want to stay here to get revenge on Gar!" Abeke said. "You admit *that*."

"Of course that's part of it," Meilin said. Tears fell from her eyes as she stared down at the saber in her hands. "But mainly I don't want to hurt you again. Help me stop myself from hurting you. Please."

Abeke's jaw trembled, and she had to clench her muscles to keep the shaking from passing to her whole body. In her heart, Abeke knew Meilin was right. In the Conqueror base, Gerathon had no use for Meilin as a spy or a murderer. The moment Meilin escaped, though, Gerathon would possess her. Abeke reluctantly nodded. "We'll come back for you," she said. "I promise."

Meilin walked over and hugged Abeke. "I'm sorry," she whispered hoarsely. "For everything. You were a better friend than I deserved."

Abeke's eyes stung. She closed them tight, and clasped Meilin to her.

"I'm sorry too, Meilin," Shane said from behind them. Abeke turned, taking the boy in. He rubbed his shoulders. There was a new softness to him that was surprising in someone so tall and strong. "If I'd only seen my uncle for what he was earlier . . . maybe your father, or Drina . . ." His voice broke. Shane sighed, shaking his head. "Thank you for this sacrifice. I'll do my best to live up to it. I'll protect Abeke, and we *will* find a way to stop my uncle."

Meilin watched him silently for a moment, measuring him. Then she gave a single affirming nod, apparently satisfied with what she saw.

Shane worriedly scanned the dockside quays. "I hear footsteps approaching. We need to get going."

"Enough talk, then," Meilin said, wiping her eyes. Beside her, Jhi leaned her head against Meilin's hip. "Get going!"

Shane creaked open the dockside door. At the other side was the town's small port–it was almost vacant, filled with the noise of creaking boats and flooded by morning light. Abeke hefted a crate and followed Shane out onto the docks. Uraza paced beside her, body slung low, ears flat and violet eyes alert.

"If we somehow make it to Greenhaven, will the Greencloaks kill me the moment I appear?" Shane asked.

"You saved my life," Abeke said. "I'll make sure they don't hurt you."

"Thank you," Shane said, relief in his voice.

As they hurried along the harbor, Abeke's thoughts were not on Shane, but on Meilin. How long would it be before they saw each other again? Could they find a way to cure Meilin of her Bile poisoning?

Meilin must be feeling so lonely and wretched, so scared at the prospect of surviving alone amid the Conquerors. Abeke wished she could hug her friend one more time. As she tossed her crate to the deck of Shane's boat and prepared to leap aboard herself, Abeke glanced back at the customs house.

Meilin was almost out of view. It was only because of Abeke's link with Uraza that her senses were keen enough to spy her. Meilin was slumped inside the customs house, half-hidden in a dark corner. She leaned forward and waved, the glint of her eyes only just visible in the dimness. Abeke could barely make out Jhi's black paw beside her.

Abeke waved back, then jumped to the deck of the ship, Uraza leaping after her and landing softly on the sun-warmed wood. Abeke found she was short of breath, but not from the run. A terrible certainty gripped at her chest, choking out the crisp ocean air.

She was never going to see her friend again.

8

THE OASIS

CONOR STARED FROM HIS HIDING PLACE IN THE SAW grass as the Conquerors tried to force their way through the ostrich canyon. Irtike had buried her head in the thick yellow blades, unwilling to watch the bloodbath. But Conor, Rollan, Tarik – and Lumeo and Snake Eyes – were watching closely.

The raiders they'd seen before must have been a less organized advance force. This army was marching in unison, cavalry trotting in front and infantry nested behind, followed closely by archers. In the rear were camels lugging supplies, tended by captured Niloans, their heads bowed in misery. The Conquerors' dark leathers squeaked and creaked as they approached the pass. The ostriches had bravely lined up at the southern end, just like before, but their force looked pathetic compared to the hundreds of Conquerors surging along.

"Zerif," Tarik said, pointing at the tall Conqueror heading up the infantry. Conor squinted and saw that, indeed, it was the handsome man with the close-cropped beard, the one who had stolen Meilin and Abeke away. "They're sending one of their most important leaders," Tarik said. "Clearly the Golden Lion is crucial to their plans."

"There's no way that line of ostriches can hold against them," Conor said. "All we can do is hope that Briggan and Essix have already managed to get the talisman before the Conquerors reach the oasis."

Rollan peered miserably at him. Conor felt his brow dotting with nervous sweat.

"That's what I was trying to tell you," Rollan said. "I don't think Briggan and Essix are going to get the Golden Lion. They were in serious trouble when you pulled me away. I need to go back into Essix's mind."

"Trouble?" Conor said, his stomach going tight. "What trouble?"

Tarik frowned. "We'll have to risk sending you back. Go on, Rollan. We'll figure out what to do here."

Immediately, Rollan closed his eyes. Conor watched as his body went limp, and his eyes began to move rapidly beneath the lids. The boy made little gasps. They'd have to wait for him to return with something concrete to report. For good or for bad.

In the meantime, Conor turned his attention back to the Conquerors in the pass.

The first horsemen reached the line of ostriches. Like the last group of Conquerors, they marched forward resolutely, and like the last group of Conquerors, they were felled as soon as they reached the birds. The ostriches' powerful feet smashed in their helmets with amazing accuracy. The riders hit the canyon wall and didn't get back up. Their horses scattered, some forward through the ostriches and others back into the infantry's ranks.

It was no accident, Conor decided, that Zerif was leading a deeper line – he was more than willing to let his soldiers take the first hit. When the first group crumpled and the ostriches were preparing to attack again, Zerif shouted a command.

The lines of soldiers stopped, the archers readied their bows, and they released a volley.

The ostriches whirled in confusion, then began to fall. It was all over in seconds: The surviving ostriches scattered, and the Conquerors poured through the pass. Zerif galloped forward to take the head. He shouted triumphantly as he led his army toward Cabaro's oasis.

Conor wanted to run down and attack, but he and his friends had no chance against such a large force, especially without Briggan and Essix. Being reminded of Briggan's absence made Conor want to bury his head in his arm – it was like he was missing a piece of himself. But instead he held his head high. His companions needed him. Briggan needed him.

It took at least half an hour for the Conqueror army to pass through the narrow bottleneck. They strode right into the desert, kicking up a cloud of yellow dust that plumed high into the sky.

As the last Conquerors passed into the desert, Irtike pressed her ear to the ground, gripping Snake Eyes tightly to her chest.

"What is it?" Conor asked. The slender girl made a silencing gesture.

Finally she spoke. "The men the ostriches killed. Their horses scattered, but they've calmed now and are gathering on the other side of the cliff, just out of view. I can sense the vibrations of their hooves."

Conor looked at Tarik, sudden hope wetting his eyes. "If we go on horseback, and there's only four of us, maybe we can outpace them."

Tarik was already on his feet. "Let's move."

Conor looked at Rollan, laid out flat on the grass, lips moving as he followed Essix in his mind. "What about Rollan?" he asked. "We can't leave him behind."

"Of course not," Tarik said. And with that, he hefted Rollan and carried him down the bluff, holding the boy gently in his arms, like a sick child. Conor and Irtike rushed to stuff their belongings into their packs and then followed Tarik down.

They caught up just as he reached the horses, which were precisely where Irtike had said they'd be, chewing at a stand of dried grass at the desert's edge. Conor looked at their small companion with new appreciation.

Tarik laid Rollan on his belly across the back of the horse with the gentlest-looking face, then fastened the saddle straps over the boy's back. Conor picked a steed and fitted his pack to the saddle. Irtike removed the saddle from hers and nimbly clambered on.

They trotted at first, until they saw that none of the mass of Conquerors ahead of them was dropping back to investigate. Once they knew they were relatively safe, they began to gallop. Tarik steered them at a wide angle so they could go around the enemy army.

As they turned, Rollan's body began to slide from the

saddle, until his head was hanging over the side of the horse. Worried for his friend's safety, Conor nearly called for a stop. But then he saw Rollan groggily shake his head and yelp in surprise as he opened his eyes to sand streaming past.

"Welcome back!" Conor yelled over the wind, grinning at Rollan.

Grumbling loudly, Rollan edged himself back up his horse, and managed to unstrap himself even while riding forward. Finally he was right-side up, galloping alongside them. "I've never particularly liked horses!" he called.

His nag whinnied in response.

"I'm not sure they like you either," Conor retorted.

"Let me tell you what I've found out about Briggan and Essix," Rollan yelled. Tarik and Irtike fell into line, the better to hear while they rode.

"Briggan's alive," Rollan said. "He faced Cabaro, but the lion was too lazy to fight. He sent his lionesses after him. Briggan might have managed it, except a group of wild dogs attacked him from behind. Not even Briggan's command over canines could shake Cabaro's hold on them."

"No!" Conor cried. "Is he okay?"

Rollan nodded grimly. "Just. Essix picked off enough of the dogs that Briggan stayed on his feet. But he had to retreat. He's hidden somewhere in the oasis. Essix rose into the air when he fled. She can't see him anymore."

"And the Golden Lion?" Tarik yelled.

Rollan took a moment to rebalance himself as they surged forward, pressing the balls of his feet hard into his stirrups. "Cabaro's still got it."

"For now," Irtike said. "I'm sure he has no idea that a Conqueror army is about to descend on his precious animal oasis."

Rollan closed his eyes for a moment, then whipped them open and visored his eyes against the sun hanging in the southern sky. "Essix is on her way toward us."

"Tell her to stay there!" Conor begged. "Ask her if she can spy any sign of Briggan."

"I can't communicate with her like that," Rollan said. "But I think something's wrong." He clenched the reins in his hand and closed his eyes. His brow furrowed. "Wait!" His eyes snapped open again, wild with fear. "There are more Conquerors coming through the pass behind us! A hundred or so."

Fear tingled along Conor's spine. His horse seemed to sense his anxiety, and swerved off course. Conor had to pull hard on the reins to get it back in formation.

Conor whirled in his saddle. Behind them, he could see a mass at the northern horizon, ringed in rising dust. An undulating, jet-black figure slithered at the head. It looked small now, but was quickly getting larger. It was a snake, and there was only one giant snake that he knew of.

Gerathon.

Conor faced forward, toward the other contingent of Conquerors.

"We're trapped," Tarik said, voicing Conor's thoughts. "They have us in a vise."

"Head for the oasis!" Conor said. "Out here we're easy targets. We have to find some cover."

"And then all we have to do is beat away a few dozen

wild dogs and lions!" Rollan called. "Make sure you keep the Slate Elephant against your skin, Conor. Without his extra size, Briggan would already have fallen."

It seemed to Conor that the wild dogs and lionesses were the least of their difficulties when they had Gerathon to contend with. And Zerif. Not to mention a few hundred Conqueror soldiers.

Essix plummeted beak-first, extending her wings just in time to slow and land on Rollan's shoulder. Rollan barely seemed to notice as he peered forward. "There's a stand of trees shaking in the oasis, toward the left side. That's probably where Briggan is. If we ride all out, we should get there before the first Conquerors do."

They didn't need to voice their agreement. Tarik directed his horse slightly to the side, and before long the oasis was in plain view. Conor's heart leaped when he saw a large gray form whirling at the eastern edge. Several small brown shapes corralled Briggan, so that he was half in the desert and half out of it.

They sped toward the harried wolf, Conor brandishing his hand ax and preparing to attack. But as they got closer he saw that the wild dogs weren't venturing past the tree line. Briggan faced the pack from the sand, but they held tight at the edge of the oasis, whining and nipping the air.

Briggan spotted Conor as they neared. His tail began to wag, and Conor laughed joyfully in response. But then he saw the severity of Briggan's wounds. Because of his thick fur, it was impossible to see the individual gashes, but Briggan's coat was matted and red in more places than it wasn't.

"I wish we had Jhi here," Conor said as they dismounted beside Briggan. Instantly the giant wolf was nuzzling him, pressing his wet nose into the boy's side, almost knocking him over. Heedless of the blood, Conor ran his hands through Briggan's fur. He tried to keep his voice calm, for Briggan's sake. "You need healing." Unable to hold back anymore, Conor threw his hands around Briggan's leg. "Oh, I've missed you!"

Now that the others were here, the dogs retreated into the oasis, growling and snapping. Briggan slumped to the ground while Tarik investigated his wounds. "Surface, mostly," he said. "I think he's going to be okay. But he's exhausted past his limits, and won't be recovering anytime soon."

Conor pressed his face against the wolf's snout. "You hear that? You need to rest some."

"Well, I wish we could offer him some bedtime," Rollan said, staring at the dust cloud kicked up by the Conqueror army as it poured into the oasis a quarter mile away. "But time is what we don't have. Either we convince Cabaro to give us the Golden Lion, or we surrender it to the Conquerors."

Irtike pointed to the trail of fallen trees that Briggan had created while he'd been chased by the wild dogs. "That's the way the dogs retreated," she said. "I think we can assume there's where we'll find Cabaro. I'm picking up heavy vibrations from the center."

Conor nodded. "Let's go."

Briggan led the way, limping gingerly through the trail of broken trees. Still magnified by the Slate Elephant, he stepped over even the largest fallen trunks. The others had a harder time of it. They left their horses at the edge and proceeded on foot, as there was no way their mounts could pass through the dense jungle.

At one point Briggan had to lift them over a tree one by one, tenderly biting into the scruffs of their shirts and carrying them over like pups. The sight of big Tarik helpless in Briggan's jaws would stick with Conor for a long time. Even in the desperation of their situation, it was hard not to laugh.

Conor began to smell something he hadn't since the hut in Okaihee, and at first he couldn't place it. Then he realized – it was the same scent as the lone lion they'd encountered. Conor opened to his mouth to warn his companions, but there was no need.

Briggan was already over the last tree – they'd come to the lagoon at the center of the oasis. The still blue surface reflected the few wispy clouds that were in the sky. The four lionesses were near, two licking the wounds of their companions. They must have been exhausted by the combat. Though their heads snapped to attention when the group arrived, they didn't get to their feet.

Why did they need to, though, when Cabaro the Lion was there, rested and whole, lounging at the far side of the lagoon? When he saw the team he got to his feet slowly, stretching his head low to the ground with front legs outflung, never taking his eyes off them. He strolled around the lagoon's edge, then sauntered over to his lionesses. Those huge cats seemed like kittens compared to him. Cabaro had to be at least a dozen feet long, and moved with easy grace and obvious strength.

"Greencloaks," he said in his velvety voice. "My least favorite of all humans. I don't know how you got past my ostriches, but you should have taken the hint that humans aren't welcome here. You'd best leave, before I get really angry."

Conor wanted to speak, to find a way to convince Cabaro that he should help them protect the Golden Lion from the Conquerors. But when he opened his mouth, fear of the immense beast made his throat close tight.

Luckily Rollan was more unflappable. He stepped forward, bravely brandishing his long dagger, however pathetic it looked compared to the teeth of Cabaro.

"Yeah, well," he said, standing tall. "You might want to . . . shut up."

When Essix cried out irritably from a palm directly above him, Rollan shrugged up at her. "Cut me some slack, Essix. It's been a long day."

Cabaro rolled his golden eyes. "The Essix I knew was a Great Beast, not a squawking bird who does the bidding of humans. Are you sure this Essix isn't actually a parrot?"

Essix shrieked in outrage.

"Cabaro," Tarik said, standing forward with one palm open, the other guiding Rollan's dagger tip toward the ground. "My name is Tarik. We have come to warn you that the Conquerors are at the edge of your oasis, and heading inward as we speak. They will be here any minute. I won't hide the truth, that we believe your talisman will be safest in the care of the Greencloaks – but right now we have great need of your might. As we speak, precious seconds are slipping by. The Devourer is here, and

Gerathon. Please, let us help you. Let us all flee, and speak later at our leisure."

Cabaro had been listening with evident amusement, but when Tarik said Gerathon's name, a fraction of fear entered the lion's eyes. He seemed about to answer when Briggan stepped forward. The wolf kept his head low, not in submission, but in a peculiar deference. A long look passed between the two Great Beasts. Conor could only imagine what the two legends might be telling each other with that gaze.

Newly agitated, Cabaro began licking his talisman. He dangled the massive pendant from his paw as he spoke. "I can handle myself in combat – no creature that has ever lived has bested me, not even Gerathon. If she dares attack, I will pounce behind her triangular head like a mongoose, and shake until she can move no more. That will be my reply to her."

Conor's heart swelled, in spite of himself. He would love to see that.

"But," Cabaro continued, "you are telling me nothing I don't already know. My animals rove all over Nilo and beyond, bringing me news of the other continents. I knew the moment the Devourer had returned, and when Gerathon was freed, a claim I doubt you Greencloaks can make. *And* I knew they would come for my talisman. They will need it to free Kovo, whose prison was stronger. I was well aware that my precious solitude would one day come to an end."

Cabaro paced around the edge of the lagoon. Occasionally he would flash something almost like a smile at the companions – he was clearly enjoying the attention, the drama. "But I will never do what you ask, precisely because it is *you* who ask it. Perhaps I would have listened to Briggan and Essix, had they come on their own. But once I learned they were linked to humans – that in their rebirth they had become mere tools for your kind – the Four Fallen lost my support. If animals banded together and prevented humans from interfering with us, destroyed Conquerors and Greencloaks alike, destroyed every would-be Reptile King, then there would be hope for their world. But we allow humans to run rampant. Why should we be surprised when their desires turn corrupt? The world's fate was sealed as soon as humans came to dominate it. Ours has been a slow slide into servitude."

Briggan began to growl softly, while Essix struck a defiant stance, sharp beak high. Conor wondered what they were really thinking, but their conclusion was clear: They still stood on the side of the Greencloaks.

Conor managed to find his voice. "Like Suka," he said. "You've given up on the world, just like Suka the Polar Bear did."

Cabaro laughed, a strangely raspy sound. "No. Nothing mattered to Suka but extending her own lifespan. I think her brain must have been damaged from the prolonged cold. I also saw the end of our time coming, but choose instead to *live* my remaining days – to spend them in comfort and fellowship."

Rollan frowned. "Conor, is this what I sounded like that day Olvan asked us to become Greencloaks? If so, I give you permission to punch me. Once. In the shoulder."

Cabaro slinked around the lagoon, his body lazy and relaxed. But there was a flash in his eyes that made Conor uneasy. Then he realized: The lion was edging toward them.

"Watch out–!" Conor started to warn.

Cabaro sprang. The cat was high in the air, and came down with claws outstretched, right onto Briggan's back. The lion's teeth sank deep into the wolf's neck and clamped tight. As soon as the massive Great Beast impacted him, Briggan was prone on the ground, pressed beneath Cabaro's weight. His breath came only in strangled gasps.

Rollan leaped toward the giant lion, dagger outstretched. Cabaro was so big, and had pounced so far up on the back of Briggan, that the best the boy could manage was to reach his paw. Rollan's dagger sank into one of Cabaro's foot pads. Cabaro glanced only momentarily at the annoyance, never lessening his clamp on Briggan's throat. With a roar that seemed to shake the very ground beneath their feet, the lion clenched harder.

Briggan's eyes bulged wide, his mouth agape. The wolf wasn't even able to gasp anymore. "He's crushing his windpipe!" Conor cried, running forward, swinging his hand ax wildly.

"Watch for the lionesses!" Irtike shouted. The cats were circling around, maneuvering themselves behind the group. Tarik whirled on them, his curved sword outstretched. When he whipped it through the air, the lionesses paused.

Mindless with fury, Conor grabbed handfuls of Briggan's fur and climbed up his side. Hand by hand, he reached for Cabaro's pelt. The lion twisted beneath Conor's fingers, the muscles thick, hot cords within the cat's body. Once he'd reached Cabaro's ribs, Conor reared his ax back and sank it as deep as he could into the cat's back.

Though Conor's aim was true, the blade made only a superficial wound on the giant beast. Still, the great cat howled in pain. Cabaro released his stranglehold on Briggan and leaped from the wolf, his claws raking Briggan's flesh as he launched. Cabaro twisted in the air and landed in the midst of his lionesses. Conor was rocketed off, tumbling through the air.

Cabaro roared, powerful and deafening. The lazy, smiling cat was gone. This was a savage opponent, the strongest they'd yet seen, made even more fearsome by his swirling lionesses, snapping and snarling.

"At my side!" Tarik called, waving his companions to him. "Back to back!"

Irtike was already there, and Rollan joined her, shoulder to shoulder. Conor wouldn't leave Briggan's side, though. The Great Wolf was breathing but seemed stunned – he tried to get to his feet and failed. "It's okay," Conor whispered, stroking Briggan's paw. "You're going to be okay."

Tarik brought Irtike and Rollan over to Conor, and together they took positions around Briggan, weapons at the ready to protect their friend. Essix hovered above, talons out, wings whipping up dust.

Cabaro and his lionesses circled them, lunging and feinting, long teeth gleaming. Each time a lioness came close, Tarik or Rollan lashed out with his weapon. Conor would have joined them, but his ax was gone, lost in the tumult. For the moment, their mock attacks seemed to be keeping the lions at bay – just. But Conor started hearing something that alarmed him: Wild dogs were yipping at their backs.

"Dogs too? This is impossible!" Rollan said, just loudly enough for his companions to hear. "We don't stand a chance!"

"Retreating is not an option," Tarik said. "None of us could outrun any of the lionesses."

His companions covering him, Conor inspected the deep gashes on Briggan's neck. Tears of worry and anger dotted his eyes. "Briggan's hurt badly."

Conor's vision swam as he looked at his hands. They were soaked in bright red blood. Briggan's blood.

"He must go into his dormant form," Tarik ordered. "Now. Before he bleeds out here."

Conor nodded. He focused his energy and stared deep in to Briggan's panicked eyes, begging him to go. Then, with a familiar searing snap, Briggan was gone, back to a tattoo on Conor's arm.

One of the lionesses whirled, looked at the jungle's edge, and gave a startled cry. Irtike followed her gaze and, Snake Eyes in hand, closed her eyes. "Gentlemen," Irtike said softly, her focus in the trees, "our situation is about to get much worse."

9

THE PLAN

MEILIN WAS SURROUNDED BY DEPRESSED RATS.

She didn't know how many hours she'd sat motionless in the corner of the dank abandoned customs house, hidden away against a wall of slimy rotten wood, the rats skittering near. Once they'd gotten close to Meilin and Jhi, though, each one seemed to give up on moving, and lay flat on the floor. Meilin knew this was probably Jhi protecting her by pacifying them, but it seemed as if the rats felt the sadness coming from the girl, and were struck motionless by the weight of it.

On the other side of the thin walls, Meilin could hear running feet, urgent conversations, and the creaks and groans of ships being manned for sea. But no one had come inside and found her yet. She was still alive.

The customs house stayed silent. The floor was damp and smelled faintly of past cargoes, of oily fish and quicklime and spilled ale. There were lines of grime on the floor around the crates, and the sawdust on the ground was dotted with mold.

Jhi sat on the floor with her back to Meilin, who was picking absently through the panda's coarse hair, removing any bits of dirt she came across. Meilin wished she could do something to help Abeke – but only the speed of their ship would determine Abeke and Shane's fate now. There was nothing Meilin could do about that.

But it wasn't truly Abeke who Meilin was thinking about now. Meilin had seen plenty of people fall in recent months, but strangely, Drina's death tormented her most of all.

First was the terrible swiftness of it. Drina had gone from living to dead in the space of seconds. Meilin also found it hard not to replay the moment of the bite over and over – those fangs had sliced the thin skin of Drina's wrist like a knife. The girl might have died from the blood loss even if the poison hadn't been so lethal.

As if sensing Meilin's dark thoughts, Jhi swung her head around and caught her gaze. The panda's silver eyes drooped at the corners. Meilin avoided Jhi's melancholy stare.

Because what struck her most was the fact that Drina had been killed by her own spirit animal. Meilin had no idea what went on in a spider's mind, but the animal had been bonded to Drina. Gerathon's influence had been enough to subvert the spirit animal bond – something deep and primal and sacred. If Gerathon could force a spirit animal against its owner, then the serpent could make someone who was poisoned by the Bile do anything.

Someone like Meilin.

Could Gerathon turn her against Jhi? She wouldn't know until she woke up from a dream and found out after the fact, discovered the panda wounded or dying by her side. Meilin realized with a start that it was only a matter of time before Gerathon used her mental link to track her down; that meant she had only a short time before she'd be caught.

She had to act now.

"Jhi," Meilin whispered. "We passed an armory when we were fleeing. We're going back there."

When Meilin got to her feet, the rats stood as well, shook their heads groggily, and limped away into nearby crates. Then Jhi got up to all fours. There was excitement in the panda's eyes – finally, they were fighting back.

Breath held, Meilin cracked open the door to the docks, then let it close again. She had no intention of getting herself captured the moment she walked out of the customs house. A trio of guards was right at the waterfront, staring out to sea with a spyglass. Meilin figured it was a good sign if they needed a spyglass to see Abeke and Shane.

"Jhi, I need you to go dormant. You're too big. You'll attract attention."

The panda looked at her placidly, her only motion one long blink.

"Jhi," Meilin said warningly, "go dormant *this instant*."

Jhi flicked one ear at her, and her head rocked to one side.

"Did you just *shake your head*? At the daughter of General Teng of Zhong?"

Jhi only stared.

"Fine!" Meilin said. She pressed her will around Jhi. The panda took on an even more mournful look, her essence squeezed tight, and then she disappeared into her tattoo.

"I'm sorry, Jhi," Meilin said, shaking her head, keenly aware of the trespass she had just made. "It's for the best." Her father used to say those words to her, when work was going to take him away for weeks. Always with love. Meilin gritted her teeth.

She knew those soldiers would only keep their attention trained on the sea for so long – she had to move. Meilin opened the rickety door again, wincing when the corroded joints squeaked. The men still had their backs to her. She slipped along the side of the building, away from the docks.

Just like in the outposts of Zhong, the manor's armory was within its walls, so guards could easily arm themselves while they defended their leaders. That meant Meilin would have to pass back up the alleys of the city's derelict shops and houses and find a way through the portcullis gate. She took a deep breath, then stole forward.

She did as Rollan had once instructed her, following the technique he'd learned during his Amayan street rat days: run along a wall, slow at the corner, peer around, then run along the next wall. It was the split seconds between walls that were dangerous. Most thieves got nabbed in the open space between corners. As she sprinted and paused, sprinted and paused, Meilin imagined Rollan was with her, his pace matching hers. She might have received more formal training than he had, might have more breeding and etiquette, but right here, right now, he would have outclassed her. Meilin desperately wished he could be alongside her.

It wasn't hard to tell when a Conqueror was coming near – they moved heedlessly through their stronghold, heeled boots clomping. With plenty of advance warning, Meilin was able to make her way back to the manor wall without much difficulty. She hid in the shade of a stable and peered at the main entrance, debating what to do.

Everyone else must have been down at the port, readying ships to go after Abeke and Shane (and, they must have assumed, Meilin). Only one soldier remained at the entry, standing worriedly in the open space, his spear resting against a wall. He looked young to Meilin – a recent recruit, all nerves and insecurity.

He would do perfectly.

After making sure no one was nearby, Meilin summoned Jhi. When the panda appeared, she stared at Meilin balefully. "I'm sorry I forced you away," Meilin said curtly, "but you don't sneak well. You just don't. It's a fact."

While Jhi continued her accusing stare, Meilin pointed at the guard and whispered, "Can you calm him? Just so he doesn't attack me right away. Please do that for me."

Jhi looked at her with what Meilin thought was distrust, and it made her heart quake. Then the panda sighed and noiselessly padded out of the shadows. The guard saw her, opened his mouth to yell, then went strangely limp. His knees bent and his arms hung at his side, hands open, the sword clattering to the ground. He looked like a kid who had come across a fluffy bunny and melted at the cuteness of it.

Steadying her breath, Meilin stepped out of the shadows and joined Jhi.

At first the guard stayed relaxed. Then his face contorted and he picked up his sword, advancing on Meilin and Jhi. Meilin let him come, her hands at her sides.

She felt Jhi's eyes on her and knew the panda was relaxed; this soldier was nothing Meilin couldn't handle. But when the girl continued to hold still, Jhi's usually serene eyes flickered with fear. When the boy was almost within striking distance and Meilin hadn't yet crouched into a fighting stance, Jhi cast her gaze back to the Conqueror, probably working her hardest to calm him again.

The guard stepped closer, sword outstretched.

Meilin knew she had to fight him if she wanted to get to the armory. But suddenly, faced with this nervous boy not much older than herself, she couldn't bring herself to do it. How could she kill someone who was doing his duty? After her own betrayal, nothing was as clear as it once was, and without that clarity, her resolve wouldn't tighten into the will to fight.

The soldier raised his sword.

Jhi roared. Meilin startled. She'd never heard the sound from the panda before. Then Jhi was on her back legs, mouth open, teeth bared. The roar became louder, then Jhi slammed down on the soldier, swiping with her paw. Her claw caught him in the middle of his chest, and he sprawled back, skidding across the sandstone floor. He was out cold.

The panda got back to all fours, breathing heavily. Her breathing slowed, and she regained her usual composure.

"Jhi," Meilin said, staring at Jhi with her mouth wide open. "What just happened?"

She gave Meilin a long look, as if to say, *Well, you weren't going to do anything.*

Meilin looked at her companion with newfound wonder, then tilted her head. Footsteps approached – she was running out of time. Meilin ducked through the entranceway and into the shaded edges of the courtyard, Jhi tailing close beside her.

Pressed against the inside of the manor's wall was a narrow stone structure with an angled thatch roof. The iron-banded door was ajar, and through the portal Meilin could see a halberd. Its curved blade caught a glint of the midday sun.

She and Jhi skirted the wall and ducked inside, Jhi's wide backside only just managing to fit through. Meilin pressed the door nearly closed, leaving it ajar only enough so that a stray beam of sunlight illuminated the interior.

Jhi looked enormous in the narrow armory. The panda sat in the middle of the room and gazed around wonderingly, holding her forelimbs tight to her chest so they didn't knock over the racks of weapons. Meilin too scanned over the contents. The quality wasn't nearly as high as Zhongese weapons – even in the dim light she could see rust along the blades – but there was a broad range to choose from. Some Niloan spears, probably seized from conquered villages, and plenty of weapons the Conquerors must have brought from Stetriol. Polearms lined one wall, crossbows another, and swords the last. Dangling above it all were the secondary tools of war: shields and caltrops, scabbards and sharpening stones. Jhi followed Meilin's eyes as they wandered around the armory, taking in all the options along with her companion.

Meilin paced the walls, fingertips trailing the shaft of a poleax, the trigger of a crossbow. Then she found something that would suit her purpose. Gracefully boosting herself atop a weapon rack, she reached high along the wall. The item she wanted was almost out of reach, and straining for it made a quiver clatter to the ground. Meilin flinched, going still, but a moment later she stretched again and just managed to snag it.

As Meilin pounced back to the floor, Jhi squinted at her. Then she saw what Meilin was holding and lumbered forward, growling again. Meilin wondered at the panda's new assertive side, but figured her own unusual behavior was probably bringing it out.

"Stop, Jhi," Meilin said softly. "I have to do this. You understand why."

Jhi hesitated, then took another step forward. "Jhi," Meilin said warningly, "don't try to block me."

Baffled and sad, Jhi reached out toward the heavy object in Meilin's hands and pawed at the air. Her growl began to sound more like a whine.

Meilin turned her back on Jhi and kneeled on the floor. She dropped the heavy metal device into her lap. Manacles.

Jhi tugged on Meilin's shoulder with her paw, trying to spin her around. But Meilin shrugged her off. She opened one of the manacles and placed her wrist inside, then closed it and turned the key. Jhi crying all the while, Meilin did the same to her other wrist.

She stared at her manacled wrists in her lap, almost too

heavy to lift. These handcuffs were strong, and would be very difficult to remove. She dropped the key into a quiver, chosen at random. It tinkled against the wooden shafts as it fell to the bottom of the leather case. It would be nearly impossible to free her, even if Gerathon possessed her. Then, sighing heavily, Meilin slumped to the ground and closed her eyes.

No matter if Gerathon entered her mind now. There was no way to betray her companions here in the Conqueror base, and if she was in manacles, there was no way to use her against Jhi. Mind control didn't matter if the body was useless.

Meilin was still facing away from Jhi, but she could sense the panda behind her. "Now we just wait to be discovered."

She could hear Jhi's labored breathing. "I'm sorry," Meilin said, scrunching her eyes shut, her voice hitching. "I'm . . . sorry."

The sound got closer. She could feel the panda's breath hot on the back of her neck.

"I'm ashamed, Jhi," Meilin whispered. "I'm so ashamed."

Jhi's body was warm. "I need you to go back to a tattoo," Meilin said. "So you can be safe."

But Jhi didn't budge. If Meilin wanted her to go dormant, she'd have to force her. "Even you don't trust me," Meilin said. "And I don't blame you. I've lost everyone and everything."

Suddenly there was something heavy, rough, and warm on Meilin's shoulders. It pressed, too strong to resist, and Meilin was on her back. She looked up through teary vision to see Jhi staring down at her. The giant panda's face wasn't usually expressive, but Meilin knew what was shining out of Jhi.

Love.

Meilin put her hands over her eyes, the manacle's chain heavy against her throat.

Jhi shifted so she too was laid out on the floor beside Meilin. There was barely room for the two of them, and as Jhi moved she sent a rack of knives clattering to the ground. Guards would be upon them soon.

But for right now, it was just the two of them. Some of the guilt binding Meilin's heart loosened. It wasn't that Jhi distrusted her. Jhi loved her, and didn't want her to be alone.

Meilin turned toward Jhi, clutched the panda's long coarse fur in her fists, and pressed her face into her belly. Jhi leaned over and gave Meilin's forehead small licks, over and over, like she was a panda cub that needed cleaning. At first Meilin hated the sensation of being so helpless, but soon found herself enjoying it.

"Thank you, Jhi," Meilin said softly, even as she heard booted footsteps approaching the armory door.

It struck her that she couldn't have asked for a better spirit animal to get her through this guilt – a weight that she'd been carrying since the Hundred Isles. Since before that, maybe. Meilin never forgave anything – least of all herself.

Jhi forgave everything.

"I'm lucky, Jhi," Meilin said as the door creaked open and the first Conquerors barged in. "I'm so lucky that you came to me."

Jhi gave her a long lick down her cheek and snuggled in closer, putting her arms around Meilin protectively.

10

TARIK

"WAIT," ROLLAN SAID. "YOU MEAN WE HAVE *MORE* COMPANY? Cabaro and four lionesses weren't enough?"

"And wild dogs," Conor said, looking around nervously. "I heard wild dogs too."

"I can sense something very heavy," Irtike said, eyes closed, "approaching through the jungle."

Then Rollan heard the crashing sounds too. A distant treetop trembled and fell, then another. The next one to drop was even nearer. Cabaro and his lionesses heard it too, and froze in mid-step.

Cabaro whirled in a tight circle, his hackles raised to make him look even more enormous. Conor shuddered. Without Meilin or Abeke, and Briggan too wounded to fight, they were at the Great Lion's mercy once he returned to the attack.

As more and more treetops fell, Cabaro whirled on them and snarled. "Are these more of your Greencloaks, come to help you? Your allies are destroying this fragile oasis. Hard to trumpet your goodness now, isn't it?"

Tarik shook his head. "I warned you, Cabaro. Those are not Greencloaks. They are Conquerors, allies of the Devourer. And they are not here to talk reason."

Rollan looked at the jeweled Golden Lion, secure around Cabaro's neck, then at the crashing treetops, heading ever nearer. Maybe Essix could try again to seize the talisman, but Rollan was loathe even to suggest it. One swipe from Cabaro's paw would be the end of the falcon.

They needed the talisman, but the very worst possibility was that the Conquerors would get it. The idea of Zerif holding the Golden Lion in triumph made Rollan furious. "Run!" he yelled to Cabaro. "Run and we'll delay the Conquerors. Save your talisman!"

"Run?" Cabaro said. "Do you not realize who I am? Cabaro runs from no enemy."

"Rollan speaks wisely," Tarik said. "For your own good and that of all of Erdas, please flee."

"Save your breath," Irtike murmured. "It's too late."

The greenery at the clearing's edge parted, and a giant black form barreled through, sidewinding into the clearing. It twisted and reared. Two scaled wings at either side of its head fanned out into a hood, and the snubbed permanent smile on the snake's face widened to show two fangs, long as swords.

Gerathon was here.

At the sight of the enormous cobra, Cabaro whirled, snarling. The lion was trapped – one way out was blocked by Gerathon, and the other by Rollan and his group. Remembering how aggressive the lone lion in Okaihee had become after it had been trapped, Rollan felt his body go numb with fear. Cabaro would have to attack them or Gerathon in order to escape, and Rollan knew which was the easier target.

Gerathon swayed, staring down each of them in turn and hissing. The Great Beast was so *long* – it was hard to imagine that she couldn't immediately strike anyone she wanted to hit. Behind her emerged a leather-armored figure. Zerif.

"Cabaro!" Tarik called. "Get behind us."

But anger flashed in Cabaro's eyes. He was taking orders from no one, especially not a human.

Rollan waited for Gerathon to speak, but Tarik had been right: She wasn't here to convince anyone of anything. The giant serpent reared and then, quick as an arrow, struck. The nearest lioness was trapped neatly between her fangs. Gerathon hurled her to one side. She wouldn't have needed to use her poison – there was no way the lioness could have survived that blow. Then Gerathon struck again, and another lioness was punctured. She'd killed two full-grown lionesses in as many seconds.

Except for Cabaro, none of them could hope to match Gerathon for quickness. As she hurled the second lioness to one side, the giant lion roared and pounced, his jaw clamping right behind Gerathon's hood. The lion shook his head. Any smaller beast would have been flailing through the air, but Gerathon was too massive. She was motionless in the lion's mouth, her tail the only part of her that was thrashing.

The remaining lionesses pounced on that tail and sank their teeth in. The serpent thrashed, and everyone but Cabaro went flying. One of the lionesses struck a palm tree hard and lay still. Cabaro roared with the exertion, his eyes wide with fury, barely managing to hold on.

One eye on his wounded lionesses, Cabaro strained to stay locked onto the coiling and uncoiling snake. Then Gerathon went into a rapid twist, and Cabaro was thrown. Within an instant Gerathon's hood was high above him, and she struck.

Cabaro dodged quickly enough to prevent her fangs from sinking into his throat, but the cobra still managed to bite deeply into his rear thigh. The giant lion whirled and bit into Gerathon's hood, opening a deep gash in the scaly leather. Gerathon released him, and the moment Cabaro was free he leaped away – right between Rollan and Conor.

Panicked and snarling, Cabaro lunged at Conor first. The boy managed to roll away in the nick of time, bowling over Irtike and Snake Eyes in the process. The mole rat went flying, and Irtike scrambled after him on all fours. Then Cabaro streaked for the nearest way out of the clearing, swiping out viciously at the only thing in his path.

Rollan.

The world seemed to slow. The cat's giant paw was headed right for him, as if Rollan had shrunk to the size of a common mouse. All he saw were the rough pads of Cabaro's paw, the claws splaying out like daggers, coming nearer and nearer until it filled his vision.

Then, suddenly, he was spinning in the air.

At first all he was aware of was the blazing pain in his side. Then Rollan regained more of his senses, and discovered he was at the far shore of the lagoon. Disoriented, he shook his head and tried to stand.

Only to see a large shape barreling down on him.

"Hey–!" Rollan said, and then he was whisked into the air again. He bumped wildly against the ground as he was dragged, splashing through the water. He struggled furiously, dagger flailing, but couldn't manage to connect with his captor.

"Put that thing away!" roared a gruff voice.

"Tarik?" Rollan said, astonished.

They disappeared into the greenery. "Get to your feet!" Tarik ordered, releasing the collar of Rollan's shirt.

Rollan staggered up.

"Now," Tarik said. "Run!"

They hurtled into the underbrush. "What . . . happened?" Rollan asked as they ran.

"Cabaro fled," Tarik panted. "And Gerathon followed him . . . Lucky I got you away first."

The tall man vaulted a fallen tree, and then reached back to assist Rollan. He continued speaking as they raced through the brush, his words fractured as Rollan struggled to stay near. ". . . split up. They went one way . . . and here we are."

With a shriek and a crash, Essix broke through the oasis canopy and landed on Rollan's shoulder. She called out, and Rollan stopped, searching around. Tarik held still beside him.

They'd reached the far side of the oasis. The trees disappeared, replaced by a spit of sand. A cliff face towered before them, at least fifty feet high, hugging the oasis. Rollan could tell from the relatively relaxed grip of Essix's talons that they were out of immediate danger. "We're not being followed," he informed Tarik. "And it's a good thing too, since we're trapped."

Tarik pointed to Essix. "Do you think you could –"

"On it," Rollan said. "Essix, can you find Conor and Irtike?"

"And Cabaro," Tarik added.

With a sharp cry, Essix took to the air.

"That means yes, I hope?" Tarik asked, watching Essix fly off.

"Yeah," Rollan said, wincing at the pain in his ribs. "That means yes."

Lumeo poked out of Tarik's satchel and peered concernedly at Rollan's side. "That looks bad," Tarik said. "Would you let me look at it?"

"Don't worry, it doesn't feel too bad." Rollan said. Then he looked at his torso and saw his shirt was gashed and bloody. Cabaro must have slashed him when he hurled him to one side. Only now that he was looking at it did the wound begin to throb with pain.

They heard a loud shriek from above. Rollan peered up at the sky and then back at Tarik, his wound temporarily forgotten. "Sounds like Essix found Conor and Irtike."

From within the oasis they heard shouts and clashing steel, along with the angry yips of wild dogs. "I don't hear the voices of anyone we know," Tarik said, "which means it's probably Cabaro's forces attacking the Conquerors."

Rollan closed his eyes and let his vision merge with Essix's. He immediately felt a surge of relief when he saw what the falcon saw: Conor and Irtike were alive. At the edge of the oasis they must have found a route where the ground rose shallowly enough that they'd been able to climb up to the cliff top above. They ran along its edge, high over the oasis. Every step they took near the precipice sent rocks skittering down the sheer fifty-foot drop.

"Come on," Rollan said, and took off. "At the far side of the oasis, there's a trail leading up to the top. That's where Conor and Irtike are."

Rollan and Tarik took off along the bottom of the cliff, making good time on the barren ground. Soon the cliff opened on the left, where a rocky streambed carved through. It was a narrow canyon, nearly dark, but from what he'd seen through Essix's eyes, Rollan suspected it would take them up to the top.

Rollan and Tarik hurried, scrambling over logs and bumping their knees on rocks. Essix soared above them, her urgent cries pulling them onward.

The canyon was tough going, but Rollan could sense it sloping upward. "We're heading up!" he shouted to Tarik. "We'll be out on the cliff top soon."

"Then we'll have a view of what's going on in the oasis," Tarik said, gasping as he struggled forward. From the security of Tarik's satchel, Lumeo gave him encouraging squeaks.

There was a ribbon of sky above them, slowly widening as they ascended. "We're getting nearer," Rollan said. "Just a little farther now."

Then Essix's cry intensified into a shriek. Rollan looked up in alarm. A figure was at the top of the cliff, a dozen feet above. He was silhouetted by the sun, but the outline was unmistakable. Cabaro.

"Hurry," Rollan said, dashing forward under the lion's watchful eye. But then he heard a terrible grinding sound from above.

With a loud crash, the canyon went black.

Rollan was thrown from his feet, against Tarik. Together they tumbled to the rocky floor.

When the cloud of dust settled, Rollan saw what had happened: Cabaro had dropped a boulder on them. It was jagged and broad, and would easily have killed them if it had hit directly. But it hadn't, and from what he'd seen of Cabaro's agility, that had to have been his intention. What he'd done instead was block the way forward.

"He's trapped us!" Rollan said. "But why trap us when he could have just aimed that boulder nearer and killed us instead?"

They heard grunting behind them, and skittering rocks. Like something huge was passing up the canyon toward them.

"Because he doesn't need to kill us," Tarik said. He loosened his curved sword in its scabbard. "Not if someone else will do it for him."

"Oh, no," Rollan said, withdrawing his dagger. "Gerathon?"

"Or Zerif," Tarik said grimly. "Lumeo, we'll need all the help we can get."

The otter jumped out of Tarik's satchel and circled around his feet, teeth bared.

The rumbling sound got louder. Rollan watched as a nearby rock trembled from the vibrations of the approaching enemy.

"Tarik," Rollan said. "If that's Gerathon, I don't think we can take her on our own."

Tarik lay a hand on Rollan's shoulder. "We have to. So we will."

One final rasping sound, and then Gerathon appeared from around the corner. The giant serpent nearly filled the canyon, only barely able to maneuver through. Gerathon read their perilous situation in an instant and streaked toward them, mouth terrifyingly wide, yellow fangs glistening.

Tarik took a fighting crouch, holding his curved blade in two hands. Lumeo scampered to the top of a boulder and reared on his back legs, ready to pounce. Essix landed on the boulder next to Lumeo, sharp beak open. Rollan stood with his dagger up and one leg lunged forward, bracing for impact. As much as it was worth, they were ready.

Then Rollan saw who was with Gerathon.

Around the corner, right at Gerathon's tail, was Gar. The huge man with the horned helmet strode forward, nearly as fast as the giant serpent.

It would be Gerathon who hit them first, though, and with the might of a battering ram. Her body wound far from side to side, the better to work up more power to muscle forward.

Rollan's will faltered. Gerathon *and* Gar: They really had no chance. There was no way to escape, and no way they could fend off these two. If Rollan had the Slate

Elephant to enlarge Essix, or the Granite Ram to leap away, they could use them to run. But Conor had both. The only talisman Rollan had was the Coral Octopus.

At her current size, the falcon wouldn't be able to do much more than harass their enemies. Unless Briggan or Uraza appeared out of nowhere, they were doomed.

When the serpent was only a second away, Rollan saw Gerathon shift so she was heading directly for him. Tarik saw it too, and before Rollan could react he'd lunged in front. It was hard to make anything out during the flash of impact, just black scales and brown flesh. Rollan heard an agonized cry, and realized with shock that Tarik had been bitten by the serpent's enormous fang. A savage wound punctured his thigh.

"You must be Tarik," a voice intoned, muffled but resonant behind the helmet.

Gerathon reared, her black hood nearly blotting out the sky, only a bare sliver of blue visible behind her. The elder Greencloak stood his ground, bleeding profusely from the wound on his leg. Already he was shuddering from the venom, his hands and legs tremoring. Rollan had seen such movements before. Early death throes.

"Tarik . . ." Rollan whimpered. "Tarik, *hold on.*"

Gar unfastened straps on either side of his helmet. "I've heard much about you. The stalwart Greencloak guardian, one of their finest warriors. I'll admit, I had hoped to cross blades with you someday. I'd have preferred to fight you unhobbled by poison, but Gerathon was . . . eager."

While Gar removed his helmet, Tarik turned so he faced Rollan. "Run!" he hissed. "Run while I delay them."

Gar had it off now. He had large eyes, his skin pale and smooth, pinked across the nose and cheeks by the Niloan sun. His mouth was twisted with contempt. "Though you have failed to protect these children, you have at least fought with honor. I will make your death quick."

While Gar held his greatsword high, Tarik's shudders turned into convulsions. His face, normally tan and full of life, had become as gray as slate. He blinked once, twice, his eyes flicking to the boulder behind them, only sluggishly returning to Gar and Gerathon. "Rollan . . . the octopus."

Of course. The Coral Octopus would allow Rollan to shrink and slip through a crevice. He might be able to use it to pass through the crack between the boulder and the canyon wall. But that would mean . . .

Gerathon hissed in fury and slithered forward, rocks grinding to dust beneath her massive body.

"Hold, Gerathon," Gar called, raising his greatsword high. "This one is mine. We must retrieve the talisman, above all else. You go find Cabaro."

"You will not order me around like a common soldier!" the Great Serpent hissed, her voice reverberating against the cavern walls. "I am not your subject, *General*."

"I'm not leaving you," Rollan whispered to Tarik, his dagger outstretched, so puny in the face of the combined might of Gar and Gerathon.

With great effort, Tarik managed to keep his sword raised against the enemy, its tip wildly trembling, drawing circles in the air. His eyes were glassy, but even so, they flashed with anger. "I'll be dead in seconds. Go! Don't let the last thing I see be losing you."

Rollan fished the Coral Octopus out of his bag and held it in his fingers, his hands trembling so much he nearly dropped it.

Lumeo scampered from the boulder and stood on Tarik's shoulder, teeth bared. Essix lunged into the air, doing her best to harry Gar. It was working for the moment – Gar feinted left and right, lashing out with the pommel of his sword, trying to avoid the bird's outstretched talons. "Tarik!" Rollan sobbed. "Don't do this."

In desperation, Rollan tugged Tarik's cloak toward the impassable boulder. With a snap, the clasp broke, and Rollan tumbled backward, the green fabric all that remained in his hands.

Tarik turned, sword in hand, and saw the cloak draped in Rollan's arms. An unexpected expression passed over his face. Hope.

That moment of distraction was all the advantage Gar needed. He brought his two-handed sword whipping through the air at Tarik. Essix only barely escaped the slash, feathers flying as she wheeled into the sky. But she managed to snag Gar's gloved hand as she went, and his mighty blade went wide. Gar readied his greatsword to strike again, grunting with exertion as he heaved the weapon high over his head.

With one hand Rollan gripped Tarik's cloak, and with the other he clasped the Coral Octopus. The edges of Rollan's vision wavered, then he became liquid and limitless. Suddenly weightless, Rollan slipped toward the boulder. He arrived at the edge, and when it met the solid surface his body became ooze, slipping easily through the scant inches of space between boulder and cliff wall.

As soon as he was on the other side, Rollan let go of the Coral Octopus and felt his boundaries sharpen again. He got to his feet in the dark canyon. Rollan kneeled and stared through the few inches of space between the boulder and the cliff wall. It was too narrow to make out what was happening on the other side, but he heard grunts and metal clanging against metal. Then, after a gasp and a horrible grinding noise, everything went silent.

Rollan stared at the small patch of ground visible through the crack. All he could spy was a booted foot, motionless. He squinted, trying to figure out whose it was.

Rollan gasped as a large, furious eye filled his vision. He and Gar stared at each other, breathing hard, their faces inches apart. There was no way, even with Gerathon's help, that Gar would be able to budge the boulder. Rollan was safe for now. But it meant little to him.

Because Tarik was dead.

Rollan heard a familiar chattering, and Gar suddenly whirled, disappearing from view. Lumeo was on the attack. Though he desperately maneuvered around the crack, Rollan could no longer see Gar and the otter. He heard scuffling, and Essix shrieking. Gerathon was moving too – Rollan could hear more rocks crunching under her massive bulk. Lumeo had to be more agile than Gar or even Gerathon, but in the face of their might, Rollan knew there was only one way this could end.

"Lumeo, get over here!" Rollan shouted. It was possible the otter might be able to fit through the gap between boulder and canyon wall. But there were only the sounds of continued fighting. Tears in his eyes, Rollan listened to the footfalls and grunting.

He heard an agonized cry from Lumeo.

Then there was silence.

With a familiar whoosh Essix landed on Rollan's shoulder, her talons digging in. Rollan imagined what the falcon was telling him: *They gave their lives to buy you extra seconds to survive. Don't waste them.*

It all came over Rollan fresh. Tarik was dead. Lumeo was dead. An anguished sob wracked his body.

And then, gripping Tarik's cloak tightly in his fist, Rollan turned and ran for his life.

11

THE GOLDEN LION

WHEN THE BATTLE IN THE OASIS HAD BROKEN APART, Conor and Irtike had fled headlong into the nearest trees, whipping past branches and startling songbirds that rose into the air in waves. Conor nearly ran into Essix as they fled – the falcon was diving in the other direction, to Rollan's aid, and he soon lost sight of her in the trees.

After minutes of heedless running, Irtike had called for them to stop. Holding Snake Eyes in her hand, she closed her eyes and spoke. "I can sense many feet vibrating the ground nearby," she reported. "But they're all behind us and moving away."

"Oh," Conor said. "We're safe, then." It did little to relieve him, though: If they were safe, it only meant that Rollan and Tarik were probably the ones in danger.

Irtike paused again, clutching Snake Eyes. "There are many mole rat warrens in the soil around here, and Snake Eyes is in contact with them. It seems to be strengthening my abilities. I can sense a large creature shaking the ground above us. It's on the cliff side overlooking the oasis. Something huge . . . It vanishes for a second at a time, and then pounds the ground. I think it's leaping."

"Cabaro," Conor said. "That's got to be him, right? Let's head up there. We can only hope we find Rollan and Tarik on the way."

With renewed purpose, they forced their way through the dense foliage. Irtike was the first to reach the edge, and peeked out from between palm fronds. "The Conquerors are all massed at the desert's edge, where they entered," she said. "But they're streaming into the oasis. I can't detect any up on the cliffs."

"So we'll have Cabaro to ourselves," Conor said, not exactly relishing the thought. "But we should find Rollan and Tarik first."

"Given their numbers, if we wander the oasis, we'll probably run into a group of Conquerors."

"Okay, then," Conor said grimly. "It's up to us to get the Golden Lion from Cabaro. Alone."

Irtike peered up into his eyes. "We can do it." She didn't sound especially convinced.

"We'll have to," Conor said grimly. "It's our only hope."

"Come on," Irtike said. "At one side of the oasis is a shallow enough incline that we should be able to scramble up."

They picked their way along the cliff face at the back of the oasis, Irtike leading the way, Snake Eyes tight in her hand. Sure enough, they came to an area of the cliff that was partially fallen – it would still be a steep climb, but they should be able to make it.

Irtike ascended with a sureness that astonished Conor. Her slender feet chose only the rocks that wouldn't slide away. He tailed after her, choosing the same surfaces she did. After a few minutes of exertion, they were above the tree line. Their position felt dangerously exposed, but he heard no cries from the Conquerors in the oasis, nor could he see any – their enemies were shrouded by the thick greenery. The passage shallowed out more as they neared the top, but also turned gravelly. They switched to all fours when the terrain got clogged with shards of sandstone. As they reached the summit, the vantage point was finally high enough for Conor to see the extent of the army below. Hundreds of soldiers swarmed the far edge of the oasis. The wild dogs were fleeing into the desert, chased by Conquerors on horseback.

The top of the cliff was an open desert mesa above the oasis, the ground made of dry, cracked stone. Conor and Irtike crouched behind a boulder. It was their last opportunity for cover before they emerged into the open. "Cabaro's vibrations in the earth are near," Irtike reported. "He's at the center of the mesa. We should see him to our left when we emerge."

He leaned out, and indeed saw Cabaro not a hundred yards away. Conor cautiously stepped out into the open, Irtike at his side. He had no chance of besting the giant cat in open combat, he knew, but he figured he'd try to talk Cabaro into putting the Golden Lion into Greencloak hands – maybe now that he could see the Conqueror army with his own eyes, he'd be more willing to collaborate.

Cabaro spotted them immediately, and went from a run to a sprint, heading right for them, the muscles of his long body rippling. Seeing the giant cat bearing down, Conor went numb. His empty hands seemed like feeble weapons indeed, and fear set his pulse to pounding so violently that his thoughts beat against one another. "Ir . . . Irtike . . ." he mumbled. "Run. *Run!*"

Irtike had Snake Eyes in hand, and held him right in front of her face. Some part of Conor noticed what she was doing, and figured she might be saying her final good-byes to her spirit animal. But then something strange happened. Something Conor would have thought impossible.

Cabaro disappeared.

The lion was hurtling forward, and then suddenly he was gone, vanished into the earth. Then he emerged again, scrambling out of a pit. After he'd managed to struggle out, he sprawled onto the earth on all fours. He started forward, but the ground gave out under him again. "What's happening?" Conor asked Irtike.

She didn't answer. Conor looked at Irtike and saw she still had Snake Eyes in front of her, staring deep into his ugly face. "Irtike?" Conor asked.

This time the hole in the ground expanded before Cabaro could struggle out of it. Conor was baffled. Cabaro had spent centuries living in this area – wouldn't he know better than to run where the ground couldn't support him? Then something struck Conor.

"Irtike," he said, "are you doing this?"

She didn't answer, deep in concentration. Sweat was pouring down her face.

The hole in the earth continued to grow. With a great roar, sandstone and soil tumbled into its gaping maw. Cabaro had sunk enough that Conor could only see the top of his mane as he tried to leap free. The force of his jumps only made the ground collapse more, though. With a yowl, Cabaro stumbled and fell deeper into the crumbling rock.

The sinkhole stopped growing bigger, and for a moment its edges quivered. Then the sides began tumbling toward the middle. With a sliding roar, the sinkhole filled in – with Cabaro trapped in the center. Only his head was visible, the rest of the Great Beast immobilized under the pressing soil.

Conor gingerly tested the ground. It felt crumbly under his foot, but held under his lesser weight. Cautiously stepping over the upturned earth to the spot where Cabaro was mired, Conor stared down at the Great Beast. Despite the memory of the grievous wounds Cabaro had caused Briggan, he felt pity for such a mighty animal to be brought so low.

"I'm sorry," he said to Cabaro, "but we need the Golden Lion. For the good of Erdas."

The lion glowered at him. The earth trapping him puckered and shifted. He must have been struggling under the surface.

Conor eased even nearer. Best to seize the talisman before Cabaro managed to free himself.

"Irtike, can you help me?" Conor asked. But the girl didn't answer. Conor looked at her and saw she was totally still, riveted in concentration. Sweat had soaked through her clothing. It was her power that was keeping Cabaro trapped, but she wouldn't be able to maintain it much longer. Even Snake Eyes looked tired, his little head drooping.

Almost guiltily, Conor reached out to the back of Cabaro's neck. He lifted the mane to get to the talisman's clasp, shards of sandstone falling from the lion's hair. The golden rope was surprisingly heavy, and Conor had to strain with both hands to get it free and drag it off Cabaro. The Great Beast had to be furious, and Conor was grateful to be at the back of his head, nowhere near the lion's jaws.

Conor carried the talisman over to Irtike, who was still standing motionless, lost in concentration. "I've got the Golden Lion," he said. "Let's go."

For a moment Irtike was still lost to whatever inner place was the source of her power. Then she shook her head clear and came around. "I feel . . . so weak," she said to Conor.

"Are you okay?" Conor asked.

Holding on to Conor for support, Irtike nodded and nestled Snake Eyes in her bag. She pointed to Cabaro, who was still motionless. "I'm too exhausted. I'm releasing my power over the earth," she said. "Cabaro will be able to get himself free once he thinks to try."

"Which means we have to get out of here."

"Yes," Irtike said. "Immediately."

Wordlessly, they made their way as fast as they could to the edge of the cliff. While they went, Conor wrapped the gold rope around his waist, tying it off securely. The talisman bounced against his hip.

As they approached the spot of scuffed earth and open air that led down to the oasis, a nameless dread overtook Conor. Suddenly he wasn't sure he wanted to see what was below. Sucking in a breath, he forced himself to look.

There had been a canyon running from the oasis up to the mesa, but it was now blocked off by a huge boulder. Conor couldn't see below the obstruction, but he did notice a set of human footprints heading up the canyon and around the bend, toward the cliff side.

As he stared down the canyon, Conor heard a familiar screech. "That's Essix," he said to Irtike. "Come on!"

Together they raced along the canyon's edge. Essix came into view as they turned a corner, hovering in the open air over the gap.

Down below was a huddled form that Conor recognized. "Rollan?" he called. "Are you okay?"

Rollan slowly looked up, then stared back down at something cradled in his hands.

"Rollan," Conor said again, waving and pointing at the Golden Lion around his waist. "I have it! We have to find Tarik and get out of here."

"Tarik?" Rollan said. He sounded confused, as if he'd just been woken from a dream. "Tarik is dead."

That was when Conor noticed what Rollan was holding. A tattered green cloak, blooming with dark blood, was bunched tightly in the boy's fingers. "No . . ." Conor whispered.

Rollan finally released the cloak and covered his face with his hands. "He died saving me. Gar killed him."

Conor's heart dropped into his stomach. The world felt too bright, and his body too light. He worried he might faint.

He steeled himself. Everything depended on the Golden Lion. If they didn't escape with it, Tarik's death would be in vain. Tarik's death. His *death*. Conor shook his head violently. "We have to get you out of there," he called down.

"You can't," Rollan said emotionlessly. "This streambed doesn't go all the way up. I already tried. It hits a wall."

Conor reached into his satchel and pulled out the Slate Elephant, the stone cool under his fingers. "Then use this."

He tossed it down. It rang out against a rock at the bottom, and rolled to a stop at Rollan's feet.

He didn't budge.

"Rollan!" Conor barked, surprised by the force behind his own voice. "Pick it up. *Now!*"

The shouting worked. As if of its own accord, Rollan's hand reached out and grasped the Slate Elephant, then he placed the loop over his neck. Immediately Essix more than doubled in size. The falcon's wings were now nearly half as broad as the canyon was wide.

Essix folded her wings and arrowed into the canyon, unfurling them just as she reached Rollan. Talons hooking into his shirt, she seized the motionless boy and lifted, her great wingstrokes gusting rocks and pebbles about the rocky bottom. Rollan shielded his eyes as he was lifted into the air. Essix gently lowered him to the ground beside Conor, where the boy slumped in the dirt.

"We'll grieve Tarik later," Conor said. "For now, Gerathon and Gar and a few hundred Conquerors are still out there waiting for us. We have to get out of here right away. Okay?"

Rollan met Conor's eyes. For a moment his face was blank. Then he reluctantly nodded.

Tarik is dead. The reality of it yawned right below Conor's thoughts, but he refused to let himself look into that horrible black space. Between exhausted Irtike and overwhelmed Rollan, they'd be lucky to make it out of the oasis alive. If Conor lost his wits now, they were all done for–and that meant the Devourer won. He looked into Irtike's and Rollan's slack faces. "The oasis below is crawling with Conquerors. We can't go that way."

Irtike shook her head. "There's a reason Cabaro's ostriches guarded that pass so heavily. The desert stretches for weeks of travel in the other directions. We'd die if we went any way other than the way we came. And that means passing back through the oasis."

Conor wanted to collapse. If only Tarik were here, he could hand this decision to him. But he wasn't here. Tarik never would be here again.

"Okay," Conor said. "Then we take the side trail back down. From there, we'll . . . I don't know. We'll have to find a way through, that's all."

"It's the best plan we've got," Irtike said, smiling wearily. She took Conor's hand in one of hers, and Rollan's limp one in the other. Together, they all turned around.

And saw the canyon was teeming with Conquerors.

The black-armored men and women had swarmed up

the narrow trail, and were beginning to surround Cabaro in the sand pit. Zerif was leading them, directing his soldiers to circle the Great Beast. There were shouts and confusion; Zerif probably thought Cabaro still had the Golden Lion.

He probably also thought Cabaro was still trapped – but Irtike was no longer pressing the earth against him. With a roar and a whoosh of air, Cabaro suddenly pounced from the pit, twisting magnificently in the air. He came down ten feet away, a whirlwind of paws and teeth, bowling over the Conquerors unfortunate enough to be near. The giant lion crouched on all fours, jaws snapping crazily. Zerif cursed and dropped back while his soldiers scattered.

"I think Cabaro's going to survive," Irtike said.

"And this is a perfect distraction. Go!" Conor said.

Together they streaked toward the side trail. There were shouts from the Conquerors assembled around Cabaro. Conor could only hope that they had enough of a head start. The companions barreled around the corner, preparing to race down the trail.

And nearly lost themselves in the mouth of a giant serpent.

Gerathon was slithering up the path, her huge muscular body filling the narrow space. She'd nearly reached the top when they rounded the corner, surprising her as much as she did them. Quick-thinking Essix was the first to spring into action, her enlarged form arrowing right into Gerathon's hood, where it had already been gashed during the combat at the lagoon. The falcon wasn't able to build the momentum she'd have needed to do real damage, but Gerathon wheeled and thrashed, trying to avoid Essix's sharp beak, sandstone rocks crushing to dust behind her.

"Retreat!" Conor ordered. "Back up to the cliff." He yanked on Irtike and Rollan, and together they spun and ran back up to the cliff top.

But Zerif and the Conquerors were ready for them. The moment the companions left the trailhead, they were surrounded. Zerif made his way toward them through the ranks of his men. He brandished his curved sword, a leer on his face.

Behind them, Gerathon hissed in triumph and closed in.

"Raise your weapons!" Conor said, despite the terror in his chest. Rollan lifted his long dagger. From somewhere in Irtike's bag, Snake Eyes chittered.

Was this resistance pointless? Putting up a fight would only delay the inevitable – they'd die in this battle, there was no doubt of that.

Then light came into Rollan's eyes for the first time. "The Golden Lion!"

"What does it do?!" Conor cried as the Conquerors advanced. They were almost in striking distance.

"Does it matter?" Rollan shouted. "Just use it!"

Conor gripped his fingers tight around the Golden Lion and summoned his will. *Whatever you have, show me now.*

Then Conor roared.

When he opened his mouth, a sound emerged that was far louder than any the Great Beast himself had ever made. As the high-pitched and deafening roar reached them, the nearest Conquerors fell to their stomachs, clutching their ears. Whenever Conor faced them, they were physically pushed back by waves of sound.

"Conor!" Irtike cried. He turned and saw an oversized hyena approaching. Its eyes were crazed, rabid foam spilling from its snapping jaws. The beast was cackling and lunging, its jaws almost closing on Irtike's leg.

When Conor faced it and opened his mouth, the hyena was thrown back by the roar. The noise was painfully loud for Conor, but he could only imagine how much worse it was for the hapless creatures in front of him.

With Rollan and Irtike tight at his back, Conor swept in a circle, the cone of force pushing Conquerors back wherever it pointed. By training his roar on any Conquerors that tried to rush forward, Conor was able to keep them at bay.

Even Gerathon was held back by the sound. She writhed and twisted, her body curling over itself, mashing the unlucky Conquerors trapped between her scales and the ground.

"What now?!" Rollan shouted over the roar.

"We're still trapped," Irtike said.

Conor released the lion for a moment and took a big breath, wiping the back of his hand over his lips. "Maybe we can move through them, and if I spin around fast enough they won't be able to get near enough to attack," he said.

"I have a better idea," Irtike said. "The ground is trembling from the sinkhole, and the weight of the army, and now all that noise. It wouldn't take much for this whole cliff to give way." She dug in her bag and pulled out Snake Eyes. He cringed in her hand, clearly in pain from all the roaring. "I know you're tired, but I need your help one more time, okay?"

The ground started to ripple and shudder. Shouts rose among the Conquerors, and Gerathon, despite her pain, raised her head, hood outstretched terrifyingly. "Get back!" she hissed at the Conquerors.

But it was too late.

The earth shook beneath him, and Conor turned toward the precipice just in time to see the edge pour down into the oasis below, as if all the sandstone had turned to water. The ground sighed toward the ring of jungle.

"Irtike?" Conor asked, trying to keep his balance. But the girl had gone back into her trance. Her eyes rolled back in her head as she swayed.

The hush of the falling sand became a roar. Conor watched, paralyzed by fear, as the cliff edge began to cascade away. "Conor," Rollan said, "we need to get moving!"

More and more of the cliff side fell, until it was a landslide. Conor took one step away, but his heels sank into the sand. His body was tugged backward, and he only just managed to get hold of Rollan's and Irtike's hands before he tumbled.

Above the roar of falling sand, he heard the screams of the plummeting Conquerors. Then he pitched to one side and saw nothing but a wide yellow rush, as if they were drowning in a sea of sand. The beating waves of it pounded his skin, scouring it raw. Conor tried to keep his mouth closed, hoping to keep the earth from entering his lungs.

He pivoted in the darkness, riding the avalanche of sand, clenching his friends' hands as tightly as he could. They gained speed as they went, and his head began to wrench against the tumbling soil – all it would take was one bad hit for his neck to snap. But just as he began to wonder whether he'd die that way, or by passing out and suffocating under the weight of the crumbling sandstone, he began to slow.

Miraculously, hot sun was on his face. He felt it warm his eyelids, and breathed in the sweet air. Conor opened his eyes and was relieved to find Rollan and Irtike laid out beside him, gulping in air.

The oasis was gone.

Where there had once been a paradise shielded by a cliff, there was now only a blank slope, like a giant bowl of sand. Everything that had made up Cabaro's animal kingdom – the lagoon, the trees – was buried. The last plumes of sand that were still airborne settled over the land. Then all was still.

Until it began to move.

The sand rippled. It made a wave, over a dozen feet long, and then a long black shape started to emerge, many yards off. Gerathon.

The Great Serpent was clearly disoriented. She faced away, scanning the flattened landscape as sand rained from her scales.

"Guys," Conor whispered, "we need to run. Now."

Irtike struggled to rise. Rollan was motionless, his mouth hanging open. "Rollan?" Conor asked as he staggered to his feet. "Are you okay?"

For a long moment, Rollan was still. His face was covered in sand, the whites of his eyes the only parts that weren't yellow. He shook his head, as if to clear it. "Could you help me get up?"

"Of course," Conor whispered. He pulled on Rollan's arm, and Rollan winced as he stood. The wound in his side had reopened in the landslide. Blood soaked his shirt.

"Can you run?" Conor asked.

"I hope so," Rollan whispered back.

They took off through the sand, legs kicking high to stay clear of the loose earth. Conor's whole body screamed – it felt like his skin had been flayed in the landslide. But all it took was imagining Gerathon slithering over the dunes toward them to find the will to move forward.

Essix kept pace with them, high above. "I'm realizing," Conor said as he puffed forward with his struggling friends, "that there are a lot of advantages to being a bird."

As the sand grew shallower, their going became easier, and they were soon able to trek more quickly. Conor risked a look backward. A few figures were struggling out of the sand, but they were having a slow time of it. "No more sign of Gerathon," he reported. "She must have gone the other way. And we seem to have a head start."

There was no answer.

Conor looked to his friends, and the first thing he saw was their stricken faces. He followed their gazes, worried that he'd made a mistake, that Rollan or Irtike had seen Gerathon bearing down on them after all. But what he saw was worse.

It was Tarik.

The elder Greencloak's body had been carried along in the cascading sand and was half-in and half-out. Only the head and shoulders were above the ground.

Lumeo lay still beside him. The sand had carried the otter so that he was curled beneath his companion's neck, cradling Tarik's chin. They looked . . . peaceful.

"Oh, Tarik," Conor said softly, turning away and covering his face. The Golden Lion was even heavier around his waist. He shifted his fingers over the talisman, thinking about how much they'd lost to get it. How much more could this quest possibly take from them?

"We should bring their bodies with us," Rollan said numbly.

"We can't," Conor said, hating himself for it. "We have so many miles to go, and once the Conquerors get organized they'll be on us. We don't have Tarik to protect us anymore. We need to get out of here as fast as we can."

"So is that how things are now?" Rollan asked sharply. Conor turned and saw his friend's eyes were still on Tarik, but his face had clouded over. "Kind, gentle Conor finally gets *hard*? He starts making the *tough* decisions? Now that Tarik's dead, does that make *you* our fearless leader?"

Conor's voice caught in his throat. "Please, Rollan," he rasped. "Don't do this right now."

"I liked you better the old way," Rollan snapped, his eyes flashing. "I liked the sheep boy."

Conor nodded. "I did too," he said softly. "But he's gone."

Rollan's anger seemed to deflate all at once. He dropped his gaze back to Tarik and stayed silent.

Irtike held Snake Eyes up and peered into his beady little eyes. "I can use my power to bury him, if you want."

Conor deferred to Rollan, who nodded.

At first nothing happened. Then the sand around them rumbled. It caved in, sinking Tarik and Lumeo into the earth. Conor watched, hands pressed tight over his heart, as the body disappeared.

"Thank you, Irtike," Rollan whispered.

As the sand fell in, Irtike broke her trance and faced them. "I'm not sure how many more times I can draw on my earth affinity today," she said. "I don't feel so good."

"We'll do our best to avoid it. And thank you," Conor said. "He deserved to be buried."

"Yes, he did," Irtike said. "I only knew Tarik for a short time, but I could already see his kindness and honor."

"Snake Eyes isn't the right name for that mole rat," Rollan said, petting the groggy rodent. "I'm sorry for anything bad I ever said about him. He saved our lives."

"I was thinking about that," Irtike said. "I'd like to name him Mikak. It's a word in my language that's hard to translate. It means both 'soil' and 'home.'"

"I like it," Rollan said. "Thank you, Mikak."

In response, the mole rat lowered his head and fell asleep.

"Let's go," Conor said, gently touching Rollan on the

back. "Tarik's sacrifice will only be in vain if we don't make it back safely."

Rollan nodded, wiping away tears.

"And your mother," Conor added quietly to Irtike. "She gave her life fighting the Conquerors in Nilo too."

The group began to walk away, back toward the pass that would lead them to northern Nilo, and eventually to Greenhaven. Essix flew above them, her sharp eyes scanning for danger.

They hadn't gone more than a hundred yards when Conor noticed a dark shape reaching out of the sand. "Wait, is that . . . ?"

Irtike whimpered, and Rollan's hand was immediately on the hilt of his dagger. "Gar," he growled.

"Relax," Conor said, his hand on Rollan's arm. "He's not moving."

They moved closer to the body, which lay completely still. The general's dark armor was caked in bright yellow sand. Blood had dried over a grievous neck wound.

Gar was dead.

"Tarik must have killed him," Rollan said. "Or he died in the avalanche."

"No," Conor said, peering down. "Look at this." The wound was covered in sand, but he could see bite marks all along Gar's throat. There was only one explanation. "Lumeo," Conor said, the world wavering as his eyes filled with tears. "He avenged Tarik's death after all."

"Wow," Rollan whispered. "The Devourer . . . is dead. Lumeo killed the Devourer. We stand a chance because of that brave otter. Way to go, little guy."

He kicked out, shoving Gar's body farther into the sand. As Gar rolled forward, a dark, furry shape was revealed, crushed beneath him.

"What's that?" Rollan asked.

Conor kneeled and squinted, then sucked in a breath. He tried to process what he was seeing, but it didn't make sense. What was it doing *here*, with *Gar*?

He peered up at Rollan and Irtike.

"It's a wolverine," he said.

12

SUNDOWN

DURING THEIR DAYS AT SEA, ABEKE WONDERED SOMEtimes why Shane's spirit animal wasn't some aquatic creature instead of a wolverine – he was so natural onboard the ship, with an uncanny sense of currents and squalls. Whenever they hit doldrums he'd cleanly dive into the ocean, cutting through the salt water only to emerge with a tropical fish writhing on the end of his spear. He'd ably climb a free line to get back to the deck, and kill and scale the fish before wriggling back into his shirt.

Abeke was used to being the hunter and provisioner among her friends. It felt new and strange to be cared for so completely. She found herself enjoying it.

They were lucky to be on Shane's family's ship, which he clearly knew so well; otherwise they could never have managed an oceangoing vessel with just the two of them. Truth be told, they made a great team: Whole hours would go by wordlessly, Abeke tying off lines the moment Shane tossed them to her, scaling the mast to lower the bib before he'd even asked for it. In her moments of rest, Abeke would watch the passing shoreline. The first region they passed as they voyaged their way up the continent of Nilo was the great desert, where Cabaro the Lion was rumored to live – then the jungles, and then the steppes where Abeke had grown up.

She was shocked at how close they'd been to Cabaro. The Great Lion would likely have been the next talisman her friends sought. Had they . . . Could they possibly have been close by?

It was a small blessing to have so much to do. Otherwise Abeke would have stewed. There was so much to worry about: what was happening to Meilin; whether Conor and Rollan and Tarik made it out of Oceanus; what they'd find when they arrived at Greenhaven; how to make sure she could keep her promise to Shane that the Greencloaks wouldn't harm him.

He'd been their enemy for so long. He was with the Conqueror teams in Oceanus, and Samis, and even at Dinesh's temple. It was hard to predict how Olvan and Lenori and Tarik would react to him. How could Abeke show them all he'd sacrificed?

She wouldn't have long to wait. Already there was a rim of green visible at the blue lip of the horizon: Greenhaven. The winds were low, though, and the sky was pinking. They wouldn't be able to dock before nightfall.

Shane and Abeke hadn't needed to speak all afternoon, going about their tasks in companionable silence. The wood of the deck, still hot from the afternoon sun, seared the soles of Abeke's feet as she gutted the day's catch –

dinner would be two flying fish and a few unlucky squid that had come too near the surface to feed.

When he saw the distant shore, Shane turned listless, standing at the bow and peering into the cliffs of Greenhaven, stubbled with bright green shrubs.

Once she'd gotten the embers up and the fish and squid were on the grill, Abeke stood beside Shane and looked out at the cliffs. Part of her soared with relief at the thought of Greenhaven, but worry bubbled insistently beneath. What was she leading Shane into?

"Have you ever seen Greenhaven before?" she asked.

Shane laughed. "Are you kidding? It would be the first and last time if I did."

"They'll understand," Abeke said softly. "I'll make them understand."

Shane closed his eyes, the lids pink-orange in the reflected sunset. "I love that you think so. That you have that much faith about people."

"Hey," Abeke said. "You were raised to believe that your uncle was doing the right thing. It was all you knew from the time you were a child. How could you have seen what the Conquerors were doing when you were *inside* it?"

"Yeah," Shane said. "I guess you're right."

"It was like my family," Abeke said. "I'd always suspected that my father liked Soama more than me, that he always expected lesser things from me. But I didn't know it was true until I summoned Uraza. I know now that in that moment my father should have been proud. But instead he was suspicious. You helped me see that I was special, even when I couldn't."

Shane turned to Abeke. The fading sunlight lit the fine lines of his brow, his nose, his throat. Abeke swallowed. "People can change," she said. "And the Greencloaks are no different. They'll see what you've done to help. They'll hear what Gar did to your sister, and they'll understand why you've come to our side."

"You really are amazing," Shane said huskily.

Abeke cast her eyes to the deck, her face flushing. "I don't know."

"I can't believe . . . that he killed her. That my uncle would let Gerathon do that to Drina. I miss her. We fought plenty, but I loved her."

Abeke looked at Shane, startled. It was the first time he'd spoken about Drina's death. Whenever she brought it up, he'd say he didn't want to talk. But now he was finally opening up, and she was honored that he'd started feeling safer with her. "It's terrible, Shane," Abeke said. "I can't imagine what you're going through. It's one thing to lose your sister, but another to see that it was your *uncle* who took her. We were accustomed to death in Okaihee. But not death . . . in that way."

"Drina bonded to her spider without the Nectar," Shane said. "And she was sick for years afterward. Back then, I took care of her every day. She was such a strong person, I think sometimes she resented me for her own weakness. That was why she took the Bile, to cure her bonding sickness. But ever since then, she was . . . defensive. She came on too strong, even when she didn't need to. I tried to convince her that she was overstepping her bounds around Gerathon, but she was tired of me taking care of her. Instead, she blundered forward in her usual way, taking on more than she could handle."

Shane let out a deep breath. It sounded like one he'd been holding for a long time. "I'd have made a similar mistake eventually, and it would have been the end of me. I . . . hope I'm doing the right thing. What other choice do I have?"

Abeke laid her hand on his forearm. It was strong and warm, the hairs bright golden blond and the skin pink from sunburn. "You did. I owe you my life for the decision you made."

"Your friends should imprison me," Shane said. "If I were in their position, that's exactly what I'd do."

Abeke smiled encouragingly. "Maybe they will, for a few days. But I'll come take care of you, like you've cared for me. They're good people, and once they understand where you're coming from, they'll relent. The Greencloaks are merciful."

"I hear what you're saying, but all the same I can't really feel it. I'll have to let your faith stand in for mine," Shane said.

Abeke nodded, staring at the skyline. Greenhaven was getting larger on the horizon, a beautiful clean square of pebble gray, gleaming in the twilight. "I wish we could go ashore tonight," Abeke said. "But the docks are unlit, and I'm afraid that if we arrive in the dark, a guard might hurt us before we can explain. I want them to know we're not sneaking up on them."

"It's okay," Shane said. "What's one more night, right?"

They dropped anchor a few hundred yards from the

castle walls, and ate their grilled dinner as the sun fell. The stars gradually emerged, their bright swaths more familiar to Abeke by now than the constellations of her old home, far to the south. Abeke remembered the evenings she'd stood watch for her companions, Uraza at her side. The leopard had sat bolt upright throughout the night, peering into the sky.

Once they finished their meal, Abeke summoned Uraza and gave her the remainder of the fish. Shane hadn't summoned his wolverine the whole time they'd been on the ship – apparently it got distressed around water. Abeke suspected that maybe Shane's connection to Renneg was weaker than he'd care to admit. Perhaps his reassurance wasn't enough to keep the creature calm on the boat. Not wanting to embarrass him, she didn't force the issue, and kept Uraza in dormant form more often than not.

Abeke ran her fingers through Uraza's sleek fur and stared deep into her purple eyes. Uraza conspicuously avoided looking at Shane. "It's okay," Abeke said, "we can trust him now."

Uraza allowed herself to check out Shane, then returned her gaze haughtily to Abeke. Evidently she wasn't as sure.

Stroking the leopard, Abeke's thoughts wandered to the next morning. With luck it would only be a few hours before she'd see everyone again. She couldn't wait to embrace them, tell them all that had happened, and get working on a plan to rescue Meilin. She wondered how it would feel with Shane there – Rollan especially would lay into the former Conqueror, but Conor would probably come to understand. They all would.

13

FUNERAL

TARIK'S FUNERAL WAS HELD IN THE GREAT HALL OF Greenhaven. It was a brilliant, sunstruck morning, and as the sun rose in the sky, its light cascaded through the open circle in the roof, pooling golden light around Tarik's ceremonial sarcophagus. Olvan had initially placed Conor and Rollan at the front of the assemblage, in a position of honor, but Lenori, with her usual wisdom, had quietly ushered the boys to the back of the hall so they could grieve in more privacy. "You've been through so much," she'd said. "If you need to leave during the ceremony, it will be easier this way."

At first Conor hadn't felt the need to move to the back, and had done so only for the sake of Rollan, who still seemed dazed after their trials in Nilo. But now, as the ceremony entered its second hour, he was glad to be at the rear. His head nodded while the Greencloaks came up one by one to praise Tarik's accomplishments. He'd had one good night's sleep in a familiar bed, yes, but it had still been less than twenty-four hours since they dragged themselves into Greenhaven, the boys' skin still red and scratched from the whipping sands of Nilo.

He wished Irtike were there with them – he'd come to rely on her quiet, confident presence. But though she promised to come to Greenhaven eventually, she'd decided to stay in Nilo for the time being. When they'd said goodbye at the shore, Irtike had headed north toward Okaihee. It was for the best – Pojalo would have need of her powers if he hoped to keep his people safe.

Thinking of Irtike, though, brought back all the dark times in Nilo as well. Conor couldn't prevent his mind from summoning the terrifying sight of Gerathon bearing down, fangs glistening. Or Gar's corpse, and the sad final image of Tarik and Lumeo sinking into the earth. The sarcophagus at the front of the great hall was partially open, to show that it was empty. It was only a symbol.

The great hall had been Tarik's favorite spot in all of Greenhaven. Conor had often found him here daydreaming, about what, he never thought to ask. It was appropriate that this was where they held the ceremony that would celebrate his life. Greencloak after Greencloak went up to the front dais to speak.

Monte, who'd renewed his oaths after Barlow's death during the Arax mission, told the story of when Tarik had cornered him in his shop at Boulder City, acting out each part. He did an excellent Tarik impression, bringing his voice low and softly accenting the ends of his sentences. Scrubber, his raccoon, flailed and squirmed on the ground, pretending to be Monte himself. It was a light moment in the funeral, and set the whole audience laughing.

Lishay was laughing long after the rest of the assembled

had stopped. She'd made the long trip from Pharsit Nang to be present, despite the danger of escaping Conqueror-occupied Zhong. When she spoke, the room quieted, and she told her own story of their time together as Greencloak recruits, when Tarik had once left their jerky behind at camp, accidentally grabbing a piece of old tree bark instead. He was so stubborn, she said, he chewed the thing for a whole day. Despite his fatigue, Conor found himself laughing and crying at the same time, great tears of mourning rolling down his smiling face.

Rollan, though, held silent throughout the ceremony. Conor cut nervous glances at his friend, who watched, glassy-eyed, while the various Greencloaks spoke. Conor nudged him from time to time, just to make sure he'd react. Rollan batted his friend away and hunched down, staring forward with his chin cupped in his hands.

Finally it was Olvan's turn to speak. The burly leader of the Greencloaks stood before them all, dwarfed only by his enormous moose spirit animal, which clomped behind him on the dais. He paused for a long moment before his bellowing voice began to reverberate in the great hall, all the way up to the cloudless sky. "When we lost Tarik," he orated, "we nearly lost our hearts. His quiet dignity and wise leadership exemplified the foundations upon which all our work rests. But let us remember that his life and Lumeo's were given to an end. For now, thanks to his efforts – and those of Conor and Rollan and our new friends Irtike and her mole rat, Mikak – another talisman is safely out of the Conqueror's hands. And thanks to Lumeo's heroic sacrifice, General Gar lays slain. Erdas still has a hope of remaining safe."

Olvan stepped to the head of the sarcophagus, where engraved stone laurels jutted out, and hung the Golden Lion of Cabaro from one of the leaves. Then Lishay passed him more and more talismans to hang in Tarik's honor. Olvan announced the names of each as he placed them. "The Golden Lion joins the other talismans we have fought so hard to keep safe. The Slate Elephant of Dinesh. The Bronze Eagle of Halawir. The Silver Wolf of Briggan. The Amber Leopard of Uraza. The Bamboo Panda of Jhi. The Copper Falcon of Essix. The Obsidian Ape of Kovo. The Marble Swan of Ninani."

Olvan gestured to the assembled talismans, dangling in the morning sunlight. "These represent the sum of our work. Though Tarik will live on in our memories, he also lives on in the legacy of the talismans. Without these, Kovo cannot escape his prison. I know Tarik would want us to celebrate those among us today who helped gather the talismans: Conor, Rollan, and the Keeper."

Conor felt his face flush as the Greencloaks got to their feet and applauded. He hated being the center of attention. It didn't seem right, anyway, being applauded while Meilin and Abeke were still missing.

Evidently Rollan was thinking the same thing. He rubbed the bandaged wound on his leg. When the applause continued, he seemed unable to take it anymore. He got to his feet and made a silencing motion.

The room became quiet. Rollan looked around for a long moment, taking in the crowd. Conor sensed Meilin would be proud of Rollan's newfound seriousness, and wished she could see him now. "I understand that there's reason to celebrate," Rollan said. "But Tarik would want us to remain vigilant. This fight is far from over, and two of our friends still remain in the hands of the Conquerors."

He stepped down the aisle, the slippers the healers had given him making hushed scuffing sounds on the marble floor. He approached Olvan and kneeled, pulling two items from a pocket inside his green cloak. "I present the remaining two talismans. The Granite Ram of Arax and the Coral Octopus of Mulop. The talisman that brought us all together and . . . and the last one that Tarik was alive to see. The one that saved my life."

Rollan lowered his two talismans into the crack between the empty sarcophagus and its lid. "Until we need them, I'd like to keep these two right inside here. Because without Tarik and Lumeo, the Greencloaks . . . *we* . . . never would have gotten them."

"You wear Tarik's cloak with honor, Rollan," Olvan said. "He would be proud to see you among us today."

Conor got to his feet, hand over his chest. Something about that empty space filled with two of the talismans they had sacrificed so much to protect made Conor's heart clench so tightly it hurt.

A hand tugged on his sleeve.

Conor whirled to see Lenori, her face pale. "Please come with me," she said.

"No, really, I'm fine, don't worry," Conor said.

"That's not it," Lenori said. "Please come."

Already overwhelmed, Conor was secretly glad to leave the great hall early. He shot a guilty look to Rollan, who was still kneeling at the front with his eyes closed, then let Lenori guide him out the back exit.

"What is it?" Conor asked as they sped along the hallway. They passed almost no one in the hallways – all the Greencloaks were at the ceremony. Conor could barely keep up, breaking into a jog as Lenori glided along as elegantly as her rainbow ibis. The feathers she'd weaved into her hair fluttered behind her.

Finally they were at the entrance to the courtyard. "There," Lenori said, pointing forward. "See who's here for you!"

Conor blinked in the bright sun while his eyes adjusted. Then he saw a familiar figure in the center of the courtyard, arms crossed nervously across her chest. Abeke.

Conor dashed across the courtyard, barely able to slow himself down enough to avoid knocking her down. They spun in a tight circle, both laughing at the sudden pleasure of being reunited. "You're safe!" Conor said, pressing away. "Oh, let me look at you!"

"Yes!" Abeke said. "And you're safe too. Lenori told me about your time in Nilo. I wish so much I had been there, Conor. Meilin and I were imprisoned not far away."

Conor hugged Abeke again. There was so much to talk about – including, eventually, Abeke's father and sister . . . and Tarik. He didn't know how much Lenori had told her already. But first, something else weighed much heavier in Conor's mind. "Meilin . . . ?"

"Is still captured," Abeke said. "Alive – at least she was when I left. I was able to escape, but she's still there."

"Is she hurt? Is she still under Gerathon's control? How did *you* get away?"

Abeke smiled. "There will be plenty of time to catch up on everything. Lenori said you've only just returned."

"Yeah," Conor said, nodding gravely. "Rollan . . . He's not himself right now. I hope he'll be better soon, but Tarik . . . There's so much to tell you, Abeke."

"And I have a lot to tell you. I didn't make it out alone – I had someone helping me."

"What do you mean?"

Abeke let out a long breath. "Sometimes we can be wrong about people, right? Sometimes our hearts are screaming something at us, but we refuse to listen."

"Abeke," Conor said. "What are you saying?"

She turned her head to one side and looked into the woods at the edge of the courtyard. "Shane," she called. "You can come out!"

Conor could scarcely believe his eyes when Shane walked out of the trees. He looked even taller and broader than he had before, but there was plenty of worry in his expression. With good reason.

Conor's hand went to the hilt of his hand ax. "Abeke. What is he doing here?"

Abeke laid a hand on Conor's arm, stilling him. "He brought me here. It's because of Shane that I'm alive."

"Stop," Lenori said from where she was standing by the castle entrance, shocked at the sight of Shane. "Stop right there!"

Shane stood still, arms at his sides, palms upturned. "Please, arrest me if you need to. I understand why you wouldn't trust me." He grimaced. "I have no loyalty to the Conquerors anymore. Please, let me help you. I just ask you not to attack me right away."

"Abeke," Conor said, hand on the ax hilt, his eyes never leaving Shane, "move away from him."

She shook her head. "Conor. Listen to me. You don't understand!"

"No, *you* don't understand!" came an unexpected voice from the castle entrance. Rollan limped out of the gate, brushing past Lenori.

"Rollan!" Abeke called.

"Ask him about his wolverine!" Rollan cried, his dagger out. Essix lashed in from above, shrieking in anger.

"What are you talking about?" Abeke asked.

Shane looked up, eyes wide. "What did you just say?"

"Your spirit animal is a wolverine, right?" Rollan said. "We fought it before. And yet we saw one that looked just like it in Nilo. Dead. Guess who we found it with?"

Shane crossed his arms, his features stony. "I don't know what you mean. You *saw* Renneg and me together during the Arax battle."

Rollan limped across the courtyard toward Shane, his dagger at the ready. "It's no fun being separated from your spirit animal for long periods of time. Conor and I know that very well, after what we had to do to reach Cabaro. It must have been hard for Gar to send his wolverine with you in the past. So hard he decided to skip that step in Nilo. But, see, that's where you messed up. Because Gar died, and we found your wolverine with him. And his crocodile was nowhere in sight." Rollan stopped a few feet shy of Shane, his dagger pointed at the boy's chest. "Come over to us, Abeke, so we can deal with Shane."

Conor held out his hands to block Rollan in case he lunged. "I think there's an easy way to resolve this.

Shane, bring forth your spirit animal, and that will settle it."

Shane shook his head. "If you're not going to trust me now, you never will. I thought Abeke was your friend. Why doesn't her word matter to you?"

Conor watched Abeke's expression go from defiance to confusion. She turned to Shane and placed a hand lightly on his forearm. "Just do it, please. Summon Renneg. Then Rollan will see there's nothing to worry about."

Shane bit his lip. "Are you saying that you don't trust me either, Abeke, after all that we've been through?"

Abeke's gaze hardened. "Do it for me."

Rollan stepped to one side so he flanked Shane. "Summon Briggan," he called to Conor.

Heart racing with indefinable danger, Conor brought the wolf forward. Briggan sat on his haunches beside him, nose in the air and eyes alert. His wounds were healed over, gray fur patchy wherever there were scabs beneath.

"I will summon Uraza now," Abeke said defiantly. "Unless you give us a reason not to fight, Shane."

"Fine," Shane said. "I'll give you a reason not to fight." Hands trembling, Shane slowly undid the two lengths of leather that kept his tunic closed. The fabric parted at the top. He tugged the leather free and ran a hand under his shirt. The tunic parted farther, exposing the breadth of his chest.

And an animal tattoo.

14

SHANE

ABEKE STEPPED BACK, ASTONISHED. THE TATTOO OF A giant beast stretched across Shane's chest, riding the hollow of his rib cage. Its tail whipped around his flat belly, the beast's open jaw in an embrace around the nape of Shane's neck.

A giant crocodile.

It didn't make any sense. Why would Shane have a crocodile tattooed on his chest? His spirit animal was a *wolverine*. The crocodile was the spirit animal of the Devourer.

The Devourer . . .

Rollan advanced on Shane, his long dagger outstretched.

Shane turned to face Abeke, his expression unreadable. Then he thrust his bare chest toward the sky.

The giant crocodile burst into the small space, shooting forward from Shane's body. In two quick strides Shane was atop it. His strong legs clenched the sides of the giant reptile easily, like he'd been doing it all his life. A memory flashed into Abeke's mind, of an armored man, spiked helmet over his features, astride a giant crocodile at the battle of Dinesh's temple. She'd assumed it was Gar. But was that . . . Shane?

"It was you," Abeke said, even though Shane was already halfway across the courtyard. "*You* are the Devourer, not Gar!"

Shane didn't waste time answering. He and the crocodile were racing toward the gate of Greenhaven. With no reason to expect an attack, the Greencloaks had left it wide open.

"Stop him!" Conor cried out.

They'd all been caught unawares. Briggan started sprinting, but the crocodile had too much of a head start.

Only Lenori stood in its way.

She struggled to fit a dart into her blowgun. Her rainbow ibis stood beside her, but it was a creature suited to divination, not combat. Lenori shouted for help as she fumbled with her weapon, only to fall to one side as the sprinting crocodile bowled her over.

The Greencloaks in the great hall must have heard the clamor. The first few had just begun to arrive when Shane reached the open gate. He turned the crocodile agilely, the beast whipping its great tail in an arc. Four Greencloaks slammed into the wall and crumpled to the ground. Shane charged in, and within a moment he and the reptile had disappeared inside. The last thing Abeke saw was the tip of its armored tail sliding through the door.

She was stunned. "I'm so sorry," she cried to Conor and Rollan.

"Don't be sorry!" Rollan yelled. "Just run!" He and Essix took off after Shane, soon followed by Conor and Briggan. Snapping into action, Abeke peeled after them.

There was no time to let their eyes adjust to the dim corridors of Greenhaven, and the moment she was inside Abeke was tripping over fallen Greencloaks and spirit animals. She got to her feet and staggered through the darkness, following the shouts of her companions. She could hear a vast commotion from the great hall, screams and loud crashes that she assumed were from the crocodile's tail striking the wall.

"The talismans!" she heard Conor shout from around a bend in the hallway. "Shane's after the talismans!"

Of course. Shane – the Devourer – needed the talismans to free Kovo. And Abeke had brought him right to them, slipping him in past Greenhaven's defenses. Her shattering guilt nearly brought her to her knees. But she wouldn't let herself collapse – the best thing she could do now was stop the plot she'd helped put in motion.

As she neared the daylit great hall, Abeke began to make out more details in the hallway. The walls were strewn with the Greencloaks Shane had knocked over during his charge. They slumped, dazed. A brown bear spirit animal was hunched over, cradling what looked like a broken foreleg. Abeke snatched a discarded bow and clenched it in her grasp. Farther along she came across a quiver of crossbow quarrels – not ideal, but they'd fire.

The great hall was in disarray. The charging crocodile had smashed benches in its path and shattered the dais. Tarik's ceremonial sarcophagus had pitched forward from its altar, the lid half-off. Crying out from astride the crocodile, Shane faced off against Olvan. The elder Greencloak was feinting with his heavy quarterstaff, but the snapping jaws of the crocodile kept him from connecting with Shane. His moose stood defiantly behind him, but the beast's massive antlers blocked it from getting around the sarcophagus to Olvan's aid.

"Uraza, help me!" Abeke screamed, and in a flash the leopard was at her side. Abeke took heart at the sight of her companion, who, after only a moment's hesitation to take in the scene, slinked forward across the hall. Tail low and ears flattened against her head, Uraza silently maneuvered so she was behind the crocodile.

Olvan threw his body in front of the talismans decorating Tarik's sarcophagus. Taking advantage of the distraction, Rollan managed to reach the crocodile's powerful, whipping tail. With Essix on his shoulder, beating her wings to give the boy extra lift, he lunged forward with his dagger and sank it between two scales on the reptile. When the crocodile whirled to see what had happened, Essix blocked its vision, flapping and pecking.

Rollan jumped higher on the beast's back and sank his dagger in again. He wasn't doing much damage, but he was slowly making his way up the thrashing body, toward Shane.

Briggan, meanwhile, had reached Olvan and his moose. Soon joined by Conor, the four faced off against the crocodile. Essix's distraction was just enough to keep them alive – the crocodile's snapping jaws missed them each time it lunged.

With Rollan nearing Shane from behind, and three capable warriors facing him from the front, Abeke began to take hope. Every second that went by, Shane was benefitting less from the initial surprise of his attack. Abeke could see some of the Greencloaks and spirit animals that had been cast against the walls now staggering to their feet. Reinforcements were coming.

Abeke nocked a quarrel to her bowstring and took aim. Tears of fury clouded her vision, threatening the shot. Shane was bouncing so quickly astride the attacking crocodile, she'd be lucky to get the bolt to connect.

Nonetheless, Abeke steadied herself and prepared to fire.

Until Rollan lunged upward, thrusting his dagger at the crocodile and bringing himself into the shot.

Abeke cursed. She lowered the bow and stole around to the crocodile's flank. With the disadvantage of coming in from below, Rollan was probably hoping to knock Shane off his mount. And since Rollan's sword arm was his right, Abeke thought she had a good idea where Shane would fall.

She and Uraza would be waiting.

Somehow, Rollan got to his feet astride the crocodile, crouched low and balancing, like he was surfing the bucking beast. Abeke was impressed – when had he become such a capable fighter? Maybe he could take Shane down in one strike. Still, Abeke readied the bowstring again, drew it back so her thumb was tight against her cheek. Whether from Rollan's strike, Uraza's bite, or Abeke's quarrel, this battle would be over soon.

And then the room went black.

Abeke lowered the bow in confusion, blinking her eyes. What was happening?

The sunlight returned, then it vanished again. Astonished, Abeke looked up to the circle of sky, flickering at the ceiling of the hall. An absolutely enormous creature was hovering in the open space, at moments blocking it entirely and eclipsing the sun. Then it lowered, and Abeke realized she was seeing some kind of giant bird.

In the eerie flashing darkness, the room went still. Shane, Greencloaks, and spirit animals all froze, staring up at the massive bird. It had a sharp, noble prow and hooked beak, and with a start, Abeke realized what she was seeing: Halawir the Eagle. He was enormous – whenever he flapped, Halawir's wingtips grazed opposite walls of the massive hall.

It took a few moments for the gusting of Halawir's wingbeats to make its way down to the floor. The moment it did, Abeke was off her feet. The wind was so fierce that it sounded like the air itself was panicked and screaming. The squall blew her toward the wall, and out of the corner of her eye she saw even large Briggan lose his footing under the blast of wind, despite how ferociously his claws dug into the stone floor. Abeke could see Conor shouting where he was pinned against the wall, but she couldn't hear a word of it.

Only the giant crocodile was massive enough to resist the blasting wind as Halawir descended. Shane pressed himself flat on its back, gripping the reptile's scales as his body shuddered under the gusts. Poor Uraza tried to take shelter against the crocodile's side, but finally lost her grip, claws leaving great gouges in the stone floor as she skittered across and came to rest on her side between a bench and the wall.

Abeke wanted to look away, her eyes tearing and screaming under the wind. But she forced herself to watch.

Once he was near the floor, Halawir folded his great wings and landed. The giant eagle, handsome with gray-blue plumage, stared at Shane with black and emotionless eyes. His beak was at least two feet long, and curved down into a sharp point. One strike with it would end anyone.

Abeke got to her feet and saw the others and their spirit animals do the same. Essix shrieked, and Halawir cocked his head toward her, listening. Then the eagle turned his attention back to Shane.

Abeke expected Shane to shrink away in fear, but he was unperturbed. He tapped his chest, and the crocodile disappeared into dormant form. Rollan plummeted to the floor, striking it with a loud thud, but Halawir caught Shane in his beak before he fell, and set him gently on his feet.

Why would Halawir do that?

Halawir was supposed to be guarding Kovo's prison. Why was he here? And why would he catch Shane to prevent him from falling?

The answer was obvious, and felt impossible.

Halawir was on Shane's side.

Without pausing, Shane lunged for the talismans decorating the end of Tarik's sarcophagus. As soon as he had their ribbons under his fingers, he lifted them into the air victoriously.

Uraza was the first one to arrive. A frenzied blur of yellow, she leaped for Shane. But before she could get her jaws around Shane's thigh, Halawir had unfurled his wings again and beat them once, sending the leopard skittering across the hall under the roaring wind.

All Abeke could do was watch, numb.

Shane was knocked off his feet too, but managed to keep his grip on the talismans. Halawir dexterously lashed out with one foot and caught the boy's waist in his talons. Then the other foot was around Shane's torso, cradling his body tightly, and with a victorious shriek Halawir beat his wings, rising into the air.

Abeke could barely muster the strength to face into the eagle's powerful thrusts, but she forced herself. She let loose a quarrel, but it shuddered and stilled in the screaming typhoon wind, clattering to the ground. Gritting her teeth, Abeke struggled to fit another quarrel to the bowstring. She saw Halawir give one mighty thrust and then furl his wings, shooting up out of the great hall. The Great Beast disappeared into the sky, along with Shane.

And the talismans.

Essix tried to launch after Halawir, but the falcon must have been wounded in the fight. She managed to get a dozen feet into the air, but then had to come back to the ground, one wing dragging.

There was a long stretch filled only with the moans of wounded Greencloaks and the cries of their spirit animals. Then, slowly, the surviving Greencloaks got to their feet. Olvan was bleeding from a blow to the head, and brought his moose back to passive form rather than have him suffer with a broken ankle. Uraza limped, one paw held tenderly in the air. Briggan shook his head, as if to clear it of some pain inside. Conor clutched his neck. Rollan was stunned, staring down at the dagger that so recently had been lodged in the giant crocodile's hide. Then he looked over at Abeke.

She'd never seen an expression of such defeat. Even now, after the shock of Halawir's rapid entrance and betrayal, she knew that it was all her fault.

Abeke put her face into her hands.

Olvan was the first to speak. "Halawir has betrayed us. That means we must fear the worst: Kovo is free, or soon will be."

And Abeke, Abeke thought. *I betrayed you as well. If it weren't for me, none of this would have happened.*

Olvan had never been one to dwell on losses, instead always pointing them toward the next fight. But tears were pooling in the elder Greencloak's eyes. Abeke had never seen him anywhere close to crying. The sight of it set her own heart breaking.

"That's it," Olvan said. "The Conquerors have all our talismans. Nothing can stop them now."

15

AFTERMATH

BACK WHEN HE'D BEEN NO MORE THAN A SHEPHERD BOY tending his family's flock, Conor used to sit on a ruined wall in the meadow near his home, spending his moments of boredom turning over stones and seeing what lay beneath. This night was like the underside of one of those misty meadow stones: moist, deep gray, craggy.

He and Abeke stood at the parapets of Greenhaven Castle, staring out over the darkened shoreline. Moonlight played on distant wave caps – somewhere out there Shane's boat was still moored, derelict. He had no need of it, not with Halawir to carry him away. The battle had taken place that morning; the Devourer was long gone by now.

Conor massaged the spot where his neck met his skull. His head was still throbbing from being knocked hard against the flagstones of the great hall. Abeke noticed Conor rubbing his head and sighed, staring glumly into the night. She'd spent the afternoon and early evening apologizing. Clearly she was sick of her own voice.

"It could have all gone worse, you know," Conor said. When she didn't respond, he continued, "I mean, the ground could have turned into molten lava or something."

Abeke smiled, but there was no joy in it. Her eyes looked red and tired from crying.

"From what you've told me," Conor said, "it sounds like you were a huge help to Meilin. After everything that happened in Oceanus . . . it was big of you."

Abeke sighed. "She's my friend. I had no option but to love her, whatever she did."

"Exactly. I guess all I'm trying to say is that there are worse things than trusting people, you know? Shane tricked you, but that's about him – not you. Your heart isn't hard, and I count that as a good thing."

"You're being nice to me. I don't deserve that."

"Shane tricked all of us, Abeke. He brought Gar's wolverine with him that first time we fought Arax, and again at Dinesh's temple. And Gar meant for the Greencloaks to believe that he was the real Devourer. If he hadn't died, we would never have realized that the wolverine was actually *his* spirit animal. Gerathon probably killed Drina in front of you precisely to get you to trust that Shane had a good reason to leave the Conquerors. We all fell for it. All of us. Not just you."

Abeke remained silent, her face impassive. Conor picked a stray pebble on the battlement and pitched it into the night. "Of course, if you want to wallow, please wallow away. Don't let me stop you."

"Thank you," Abeke said. Then she gave a long, guttering sigh. "Thank you for telling me about my family too."

"I'm sorry," Conor said. "I really am. I feel like you and I have always put a lot of faith in our families, and yours . . . It can't have been easy growing up alongside people who didn't value you. It made me so angry, Abeke. For your sake."

Abeke shut her eyes for a long moment. "I can understand why you're angry, but Pojalo is still my father. It's hard for me to feel mad at him. All I feel is confused. But if there's one thing I'm coming to realize, it's that some bonds aren't unconditional. Sometimes the family you find can be better for you than the one you grew up trusting."

Conor slid closer and gently put his arm around Abeke's shoulder. "I think of you as family too," he said.

The torchlight flickered, and Conor turned to see Uraza standing in the doorway, her fur spotted orange in the ruddy fire glow. Abeke's back straightened.

"What is it?" Conor whispered.

"I think someone's in the great hall," Abeke answered. And then, noiselessly, she and Uraza were off.

Conor struggled to keep up, his booted feet clomping as he bolted after the silent pair. Briggan joined him on the way, and the four were soon standing at the entrance to the great hall.

Abeke held a finger to her lips and eased the door open, wincing when the hinges creaked. They crept into the cavernous space as quietly as they could, two humans and two animals, all alert.

A cloaked figure leaned into Tarik's ceremonial sarcophagus, trying to climb inside, one foot on its carved edge. Conor had his ax on him – no way was he going to let it leave his side after the day's events – and quietly eased it from his belt.

Abeke had her bow out and nocked an arrow. While Uraza stole forward, she drew back the string.

At the sound of the creaking catgut, the figure whirled to face them. Abeke's fingers trembled, and the surprise of seeing Rollan's face made her let go of the string. She fell as she did, sending the arrow flying safely into the sky.

Rollan had a hand over his mouth, shocked at how close he'd come to death. Then his face shifted into its usual mocking smile. "Don't you think you have enough to feel guilty about without killing me too?"

"What are you *thinking*, sneaking around like that?" Abeke hollered, leaping to her feet. "When we're all on edge . . . I could have killed you!"

"Not with aim like that, you couldn't."

Briggan whined, and Conor shook his head. "Enough, guys."

"I thought you went to bed right after dinner," Abeke said.

"I did go to bed," Rollan said. "And then I got right back out. You think I could sleep after a day like today? Come on over, and I'll show you what I was doing."

"What's got you in such a good mood?" Conor asked as he approached. His hand shook with nerves as he placed the ax back into his belt.

"After everything that happened today, I wasn't sure who we could trust. I didn't want to do this in front of everyone, but I have complete faith in you two, of course. Give me a boost and I'll show you."

Conor held out two interlaced hands, and Rollan placed his foot in them. After Conor had boosted him up, Rollan clutched the edge of the sarcophagus. Leaning in deep, he fished around.

"What are you *doing*?" Abeke asked.

Finally Rollan emerged and leaped back to the floor. He lifted his hand into the air. Two items dangled from it, clattering together.

The Granite Ram of Arax. The Coral Octopus of Mulop.

"We still have two of the talismans!" Conor said, clapping in joy.

"So all's not lost," Abeke breathed. She threw her arms around Rollan. "You're amazing!"

"That's what I keep trying to tell you guys," Rollan said with a grin.

"Just think!" Abeke said. "We still have a chance. If we can manage to protect these two talismans, the Devourer can't complete his plan."

"Nilo and Zhong are overrun," Rollan said, sighing ruefully. "Kovo will be out of his prison soon, if what Mulop told us is true. Halawir is a traitor, and the Devourer – the real Devourer – has twelve talismans. Even if Tellun himself bounded in here with party hats, I'm not sure there would be any reason to celebrate."

"I don't care," Abeke said. "Seeing those has me feeling good for the first time today."

Conor looked at the two talismans in Rollan's hands. They were such small things, and yet essential to the very fate of the world. The moonlight streaming in iced their edges, its gleam reflecting in his friends' eyes.

He put one arm around Rollan and another around Abeke. Together, they stared through the open ceiling of the great hall into the night sky, where a splash of stars winked through the clouds.

To Conor, they almost looked like an arrow pointing the way south, to Stetriol. The Conquerors' home.

"We have two talismans," he said. "And we know who has the rest. So let's get moving."

Eliot Schrefer is the National Book Award finalist author of *Endangered*, about a girl surviving wartime in Congo with an orphaned ape. His research for his Great Ape Quartet books has led him to a bonobo sanctuary in the Democratic Republic of Congo and on a boat trek through the jungles of Borneo. He once worked as a sea turtle research assistant and had many fish while growing up, of which only the catfish survived.